To Lillian

Vic Knight's Florida

Vic Hosylet

mar '97

St. Augustine, with a head start on the rest of the U.S., enjoyed a brief tenure as the "Newport of the South," with the advent of Henry Flagler and his hotels and rails. This was her charming waterfront promenade, circa 1880s. (Courtesy Florida Department of Commerce/Tourism Division)

Vic Knight's
FLORIDA

By Victor M. Knight

PELICAN PUBLISHING COMPANY
Gretna 1993

The word "Pelican" and the depiction of a pelican are
trademarks of Pelican Publishing Company, Inc., and are
registered in the U.S. Patent and Trademark Office.

Library of Congress Cataloging-in-Publication Data

Knight, Victor M.
   [Florida]
   Vic Knight's Florida / by Victor M. Knight.
      p. cm.
   Includes bibliographical references.
   ISBN 0-88289-964-3
   1. Florida—History—Miscellanea. I. Title. II. Title: Florida
F311.5.K55   1993
975.9—dc20   93-15569
                                                        CIP

*Jacket photographs: NASA, St. Petersburg's Municipal Pier (Courtesy St.
Petersburg Historical Society), Sunshine Skyway Bridge over Tampa Bay
(Courtesy Florida Department of Commerce), Jacksonville's Riverwalk (Photo
by Judy Jacobsen Photographic Service, Jacksonville), St. Augustine City Gates
(Courtesy Florida State News Bureau), Tampa's Gasparilla Festival (Courtesy
Tampa/Hillsborough Convention and Visitors Association)*

Manufactured in the United States of America
Published by Pelican Publishing Company, Inc.
1101 Monroe Street, Gretna, Louisiana 70053

This labor of love is a history full of people, dedicated to:

All those long-suffering Crackers who enjoy their history but don't want to work quite so hard at it.

To the dozen or so historians, authors, and storytellers who've given so generously of their time, knowledge, and material, and who've let us add their personal stamp to the results.

To you—our reader—may you enjoy your trip through the Magic Land and your Florida time capsule.

But especially to the one who gave up: dinners, shows, trips, California, Alaska—even some medium-mixed doubles—for several years. A lesser person might have given up on the author. To Patty, the one who was willing to wait, this book is lovingly dedicated.

Tampa in the 1990s, with soaring skyscrapers framing the incredible magic of Henry Plant's Tampa Bay Hotel. (Courtesy Florida Department of Commerce/Tourism Division)

Omnipresent water makes every town a special town. Gleaming white sugar-sand marks Panama City Beach, along with its dramatic entertainment tower. (Courtesy Florida Department of Commerce/Tourism Division)

Contents

Preface

This is a book about Florida. It is a book of facts. There are 973,857 facts in this book (973,859 if you count those first 2). That should be enough to satisfy almost anyone.

If you enjoy this sort of thing, this is precisely the sort of thing you're going to enjoy. That's our guarantee! Our other guarantee is: if not entirely satisfied with the contents of this book, return the unread portion and we'll happily return the unspent portion of your money. Now *that's* a guarantee! So we can well afford to give you the extra, free sample chapter, just ahead.

Another advantage of this book is that every chapter contains Absolutely New Stuff! No repeat chapters here! Nosiree Bob! Not like you find in so many cheaper, less-prestigious books down at the Cheaper-Less-Prestigious Bookstore.

The book covers some six hundred years of Florida. This is very difficult to do, since Florida only has about five hundred years of history . . . which is still two hundred years more than the rest of the nation.

Which seems to be some sort of secret.

Once you get through this preface, the acknowledgments, the "Special Reader Warning" just ahead, and the guaranteed free chapter, then you're ready to start the book.

Happy trails.

From far West Florida towards the southeast in the 1920s, there was a gradual increase in activity, developments, crowds, land auctions, busses, and buyers. This was midstate at the Haven-Villa Corp., near Winter Haven. Promoters chartered special trains to bring buyers from the Midwest. (Courtesy Florida State Photographic Archives)

The ELCAR "superbusses" brought prospects out to the new town of Hialeah, west of Miami, and on these roads, too! The Indian gentleman in the striped dress became a sort of logo for everything from Ft. Myers to Naples to Miami. (Courtesy Florida State Photographic Archives)

Acknowledgments

In a work encompassing five years of research and hundreds of interviews and publications, listing every single assist will be a challenge.

In some instances, we've made direct reference to a writer's work within the text, in addition to listing the work in the bibliography. Archivists who assisted in collecting pictures for the work are recognized under "Advisors" below. While many citations will overlap, let us try to list here the people who've played roles in bringing these pages to you.

Among writers, Jim Warnke started the work on its way in 1988 along with the late Nixon Smiley, who shared parts of his life with us. There were also Nick Wynne, Virginia Parks, Stuart McIver, Judge Jim Knott, Ernie and Jill Couch, Ray Arsenault, Gene Burnett, Patrick Carr, the inimitable Hampton Dunn . . . all have been more than generous in adding their stamp to these pages.

Photographically, Joan Morris and Jody Norman of our Florida State Photographic Archives (SPA) were of great help. We give a special bow to Dixie Lee Nims, photo archivist at the Florida Department of Commerce, Tourism Division. Superb photos came from Judy K. Jacobsen in Jacksonville; from Paul Camp, special collections archivist at the University of South Florida, Tampa; as well as from Hampton Dunn, president, Florida State Historical Society.

And, speaking of historical societies, our files bulge with material from all the great ones, starting with the State Society, Nick Wynne and Paul Camp, to Dorothy Patterson and Norma Simon of Delray Beach; Peg McCall and Susan

McDermott of Boca Raton; Virginia Parks of Pensacola; Jeannette Wenzel and Midge Loflin of St. Petersburg's society; Janet VanLiere and Stacy Rosseter of Tampa/Hillsborough Convention and Visitors Association; Melanie Barr, historic planner of Gainesville; Mary Neely Woods of Pensacola's Naval Aviation Foundation; and Kay Grinter and the fine crew at NASA.

We also thank Laura Pichard and Karen Moore of Florida State University for their help in the Wakulla Springs research, Melanie Wilbanks from the Pensacola Tourism Office, Pat Craig for her great help from the Riverwalk in Jacksonville, Joyce Allyn for all her "Gasparilla data," Patricia Treib of the Plant Museum in Tampa, Andrea Trimmer of the Belleview Mido at Belleair for their Henry Plant assists, Louise Malanchuk of the U.S. Army Corps of Engineers for the "water-planning data," Dover Publications for their help, and especially great friends Bob Hayes of Delray Beach and Marlene Ryan of Boynton Beach for their five years of help, answers, and patience in preparing, editing, and typing the manuscript.

While we've singled out specific persons at our great Florida historical societies, we must acknowledge the staffs of societies in Naples, Ft. Myers, Boca Raton, Delray Beach, Miami, South Florida, St. Petersburg, Tampa, Gainesville, Jacksonville, Tallahassee, Pensacola, and especially Elinor Perrin and Andy Hermann from the Kissimmee society for their great help in the Disston material.

Other sources and assists came from wonderful people at the Florida Department of Commerce, Florida State Photographic Archives, Florida Department of Transportation, U.S. Army Corps of Engineers, South Florida Water Management District, plus many city and county offices around the state.

Our media colleagues who've been so very helpful with clearances and information include staffers from *Florida Trend* magazine, *The Miami Herald, The Orlando Sentinel,* the *Sun-Sentinel,* the *St. Petersburg Times,* and other publications, and Clem Winke and the crew at *The News of Palm Beach County.*

Literally reams of data have come from all these people, and all with painstaking attention to accuracy and detail. Any errors and omissions in interpretation, preparation, and composing are my own. Below we've listed alphabetically those who've contributed so generously of their time and interest, their files, and their own works to add dimension to *Vic Knight's Florida*. Our gratitude to them knows no bounds.

ADVISORS

Raymond Arsenault—Author, *St. Petersburg and the Florida Dream*; historian; associate professor of history, University of South Florida at St. Petersburg.

William Beck—President, Star Publishing, Boynton Beach; publisher of Florida books, advisor, consultant.

Gene M. Burnett—Author, *Florida's Past* series; history columnist and magazine researcher on Florida folklore.

Patrick Carr—Author, *Sunshine States*; published in national publications; authority on Tampa Bay political and social issues.

Ernie and Jill Couch—Authors, *Florida Trivia* and over fifteen books on state trivia.

Hampton Dunn—Author, *Wish You Were Here, Yesterday's Florida*; eighteen books on Florida; TV commentator; lecturer; historian; president, Florida State Historical Society; eminent Florida authority.

Judge James R. Knott—Author, *Yesterday's Palm Beach* series; historian; eminent jurist and speaker; from one of Florida's First Families; family home is Knott House of Tallahassee.

Stuart McIver—Author, *Glimpses of South Florida History, Yesterday's Palm Beaches,* and other books; noted columnist and expert on Southeast Florida and Broward County history.

Sam Mickler—President, Mickler's Floridiana, Oviedo, Fl., a book distributorship with over three thousand titles on one subject: Florida.

Allen Morris—Author, *Florida Handbook*; veteran newspaper writer; historian; Florida State House of Representatives; legislative authority.

Joan Morris and Joanna Norman—Archivists, Florida State Photographic Archives, Tallahassee; dual authorities on over a half-million photographs.

Virginia Parks—Author, *Pensacola: Spaniards to Space Age*; historical editor.

Nixon Smiley—Author, longtime newspaper columnist, speaker, historian, died in 1990 but much of his knowledge was included in *Yesterday's Miami*.

James Warnke—Author, *Ghost Towns of Florida, Florida Treasures* and other books; research expert on Florida history, lost towns, and treasures; catalyst for this book.

Dr. Lewis N. ("Nick") Wynne—Author; executive director, Florida State Historical Society; editor; advisor and consultant; lecturer; educator.

Special photographic selection and assistance—Joanna ("Jody") Norman, Florida State Photographic Archives; Karen Moore, Florida State University; Dixie Lee Nims, photo archivist, Florida Department of Commerce; Judy K. Jacobsen, producer of the classic "Jacksonville Landing" photograph and president of Judy Jacobsen Photographic Service; Paul Camp, special collections archivist; Jeannette Wenzel, St. Petersburg Historical Society.

Special Reader Warning

This book is loaded and should be handled with care. You would no more handle this book carelessly than you would rip off a mattress label. It is designed for mature audiences.

When you're juggling 973,857 facts in your hands, caution is common sense. Reader discretion is urged for your safety.

Do not try to absorb all the facts in this book in one sitting; it just can't be done. Place this book on your bedside table. Indulge only marginally each evening as you retire. You will enjoy deep sleep. And quickly, too.

Set yourself a sensible quota of facts each evening. Mark your place! Losing your place can be dangerous to your health. Cases are on record of persons actually starting to re-read the same material. They simply did not mark their places. This can bring on dropsy, gout, drowsiness, not to mention a very cross humor next morning at breakfast. We certainly don't want that, now, do we! Instances have been reported of addictive readers breaking out in terrible rashes and—depending on one's age—pimples! So don't blame us. We warned you.

This material is designed for mature audiences only. It was originally to be shipped in a plain brown wrapper . . . and when the movie rights are settled, it will only be shown in a building at least twenty-one years old. We do have standards, you know.

We simply felt you deserved to know before you got involved.

A Free Chapter

This is a free chapter. Do not pay!

This chapter is a free sample. The actual book you have purchased begins on the following pages.

For some seventy-odd years, the St. Petersburg *Evening Independent* was given away, free, to everyone, subscriber and stranger alike, on any day during which the sun did not shine in St. Petersburg.

During the 1930s and 1940s, newsboys were told by the older guys that the sun actually had to shine directly on the newspaper building itself by noon, or the paper would be free to everyone. The really naïve kids were told that there was a mysterious metal plate on the roof, and the sun had to shine on it. If it did not do so (we were told), a machine automatically inserted a two-column-by-four-inch "box" on the front page of the paper, emblazoned with the message: "THIS IS A FREE PAPER! DO NOT PAY!"

The then-publisher, Maj. Lew Brown, and the eventual owners, the Poynter newspaper interests, continued the charming policy until the paper's demise in the 1980s, averaging only three to four free issues per year. St. Petersburg's sunshine was very dependable.

We trust the Poynter interests will forgive our imitation of the headline and of Brown's inspired promotional idea, which drew measurable press from all over the nation about the "Sunshine City" as well as the Magic Land of Florida.

Such genius deserves commemoration. And besides, we felt our readers deserved at least one, free, sample chapter before the Real Stuff gets underway.

Vic Knight's Florida

First came the land. Whether millions of years before Ponce de Leon, or a few months before the explosion of the land boom of the 1920s, much of Florida looked like this raw, sandy plain awaiting the developer's magic touch in south Palm Beach County. (Courtesy Delray Beach Historical Society)

CHAPTER 1

The Land

IT ALL BEGAN WITH THE LAND

It all began with this illogical, improbable afterthought of land, hung on the bottom of the North American landmass by the Great Land Creator a few billion years ago. Geographers call it the Peninsula State; travellers call parts of it a panhandle; others call it a boomerang. For heaven's sake, Italians call theirs a boot.

As every Florida depression kid knows, it is none of these. It's a pistol. The part we knew as West Florida (we hadn't heard about anything called a "panhandle" yet) was the barrel; the curve of the state was the trigger; and the bottom was the handle. The only other state even coming close was Oklahoma . . . and it only had a short, stubby, little barrel and the handle was too fat to hold.

At Christmastime, Florida depression kids would sometimes get a present. It might have been a jigsaw puzzle of the then forty-eight states. Kids would zero in on the one piece that was instantly recognizable and big enough to handle. They always knew where it went. The "Florida piece" was the puzzle starter.

So how long has man inhabited this part of the earth? Following an address, the author was approached by a charming lady who said, "Just think, back before Ponce de Leon, all

Florida was under water. . . . " Actually, man roamed the Everglades thirty to forty thousand years ago. Remains have been found beneath layers of muck, peat, rock, even bones of the mammoth and the saber-toothed tiger.

Near the town of Moore Haven, on Lake Okeechobee, an Ice-Age village has been unearthed with bones and artifacts estimated to be 17,000 years old. In one instance, a stone spear was still embedded in the femur of a giant sloth.

It is this ancient landmass, nearly 60,000 square miles of boomerang, panhandle, boot, or pistol, and its 30,000 years of history, with which we are concerned.

With 57,850 square miles of land, over 1,000 miles of coast or shorelands, and nearly 800 miles of white, sandy beaches, Florida is about the size of New England. Yet at no time can one be more than 60 miles from the nearest coast, shore, or beach. This is a situation unmatched on the globe.

The charming lady's comment was partly correct. Her chronology was only off by about 37,898,743 years (approximately).

Going back over the aforementioned 30,000 years alone, estimates show that over 35,000 Indians made their homes on the Florida landmass. They had probably made their way here by crossing over the Bering Sea land bridge and coming south, or by canoeing from Central and South America. No one knows for sure.

One thing is certain; these were the first Crackers.

And it was this landmass upon which came a young, seagoing officer, Ponce de Leon. He named it "La Florida" that day in 1513 not for any flowers he saw, 'cause he probably saw sea oats, sea grape, weeds, sandspurs, and fiddler crabs, but for Pascua de Flores, the Feast of Flowers—for it was Easter Sunday back in Spain.

By the way, Ponce also gave this "first white man's name" to all that he could see and beyond—the entire continent—as he claimed it for Spain. It was Florida's first true "first."

Now, good old Cracker Logic tells us that but for a flip of a territorial coin, the rest of you folks might very well be living in the United States of Florida. Just remember that.

And, as any good Cracker son or daughter will tell you, just remember too that the whole thing started here, with ol' Ponce. Which seems to be some sort of a secret.

Now, for you folks who are really keeping track, Columbus was busy with four voyages, opening the New World! He was exploring the Bahamas, Hispaniola . . . a whole bunch of places from Puerto Rico to Cuba. But stepping ashore in "America" was not to be his prize.

"How did Ponce get to Florida in the first place?" you query. Good question. Thought you'd never ask.

On Columbus's second voyage exploring the New World, along with Columbus's brother, Diego, was a young officer named Ponce de Leon. As explorations continued, Ponce was left behind as governor—*adelantado*—of the "Puerto Ricos." Soon after, Diego, thinking he should be governor, asked the king for the job. (Since Diego, in the meantime, had married the king's niece, the job was probably a shoo-in . . . or whatever a shoo-in was called back in 1493. Don't worry if you get lost. We'll cover all this in "The History" chapter.)

Anyway, as you probably guessed, Diego got the job, and Ponce, now an out-of-work governor, asked the king to name him governor of some islands called the Beminis, somewhere north of Puerto Rico. The king said, "Sure . . . if you can find them" (or words to that effect).

Ponce agreed to build, outfit and staff his own ships, at his own expense, and search for the Beminis, which he was to rule, if he could find them.

So Ponce was actually looking for work, and thought he had found the Beminis, when he stepped ashore on our improbable landmass—which he also thought was a giant island—on that Easter Sunday morning, back in 1513.

It would appear we owe a lot to Ponce. He did the whole project on his own money, with his own ships, at his own risk. Ponce actually discovered "America" (La Florida), while Columbus was exploring the New World.

Now we need to look at a couple of things about the name "America." (You can skip this if you're easily upset, but we'll hit you with it again in "The History" chapter.) A) Columbus did not actually name America for Amerigo Vespucci, the Italian explorer whom he admired. B) The name was first written on a map in 1507, by an obscure German mapmaker named Waldseemuller. He was a big fan of Vespucci. And it was to designate South America. C) Even into the 1530s, a demand was made for suppression of all maps containing the name *America,* which was considered a typographical error.

And speaking of names, "Florida" has remained "Florida" under all the five flags at St. Augustine, all the six flags at Pensacola . . . and all the eight flags at Fernandina. In 1845 the land made it to statehood, after 332 years of just being Florida, the oldest-named land in the New World.

EVERY PLACE HAS GOTTA
BE SOMEPLACE—LAND 101

With such a wealth of material on Florida's Indian lore available, it is unlikely that these pages could bring any new insights into our first residents.

That the Indians found the climate warm and pleasant after crossing the Bering Sea land bridge and migrating thousands of miles south to come to Florida, even before it was invented, has been well documented. It *had* to be great after the Bering Sea in February!

That the tribes settled in various areas, traded and fought with their neighbors, hunted, and fished has been certified beyond doubt.

For our purposes, there are two subjects to explore: tribal locations and language and names. The latter became their true legacy to present generations.

We will begin clockwise from the northwest. Here we see the Indian influence in the "Apalachee" names—Apalachicola Bay, River, and town, plus many Apalachee names throughout the Panhandle. And the Indian words "Talla" and "Hassee" mean "Old Town."

(In some instances, various meanings may apply, depending on which of several "tribal tongues" is being used.)

In the Jacksonville/Gainesville/Daytona Beach triangle, the Timucuan tribal families gave us names of the Tomoka region: Tomoka River, Tomoka Oaks, even Tomoka Homes.

Down the east coast, we find the town of Tequesta. The Ais tribe along with the Jaega and Tegesta families had spread through this area.

And completing our circle, up the southwestern coast, the Calusa tribal families left us (with various spelling) the

The bay nurtures laid-back Apalachicola to this day. The old coastal town has expanded into treelined streets in residential sections.

(Courtesy Florida Department of Commerce/Tourism Division)

Caloosahatchee River, Bay, Park, countless mobile home parks, dry-cleaning plants, hardware stores, and even a transmission repair shop. A powerful tribe.

Even Miami itself, settled back in 1567, only two years after St. Augustine, was "My-Hai-My," from the Ais/Jaega/Tegesta tongue. It meant "Big Water," referring to Biscayne Bay.

And now for some random place names.

In the deep south, "Chokoloskee" comes from a combination of two Seminole/Creek words and means "Old House."

Back north, in Timucuan lands south of Gainesville, "Paine's Prairie" was named for a Seminole chief, King Paine. It was at one time a giant lake (more on the "Lost Lake" later).

And back south, where there *is* a giant lake, the 770-square-mile Lake Okeechobee combines two words, "Okee" and "Chobee," also meaning Big Water.

The Indian names abound. Tribal families left us "Pensacola" from two sources: a tribe called Pansafalaya, meaning "long-haired people"; or a pair of Choctaw words, "Pahnsi" and "Okla," also meaning "hair" and "people."

Still in West Florida, the names roll on—Waukeenah, Wakulla, and Lake Miccosukee.

"Kissimmee," from Seminole, means "Happy Hunting Ground." Aripeka, a tiny hamlet in Pasco County, is named for a Miccosukee chieftain. Bertha Bloodworth and Alton Morris tell of several sources and nicknames for the charming "time-capsule" town of Micanopy, with its oak-lined ("tree-tunnel") roads, just south of Gainesville. It was named for a Seminole chief, but also is said to refer to a slow-paying Irishman at the trading post, Mikey-No-Pay, and/or an Indian who didn't pay at all, Me Can No Pay. You pays your money and you takes your choice.

As every University of Florida Gator can tell you, the word "Ichetucknee" has a special meaning. The small, natural springs in Columbia County provides great recreation for Gators, who sluice down the icy Ichetucknee River on (or in) giant inner tubes. (You remember inner tubes?) It's a great sport, especially if you're nineteen. By the way, "Ichetucknee" can mean anything from "Beaver Pond" to "Blistered Tobacco." You pays your money, etc.

We also have Osceola, Seminole, and the Choctawahatchee River (you guessed it: "River of the Choctaw"!). (By the way,

The "longest wooden wagon-bridge in the world" would span Biscayne Bay in June 1913. T. J. Pancoast stands beside the very first car across the bridge, leading the caravan in the gala celebration.
(Courtesy Florida State Photographic Archives)

Travellers on I-75 just south of Gainesville will cross giant Paine's Prairie. In past centuries it was a vast lake carrying tourists on paddle-wheelers and even on a railroad crossing to the resort. In the 1800s, the lake actually drained itself, becoming the grassy prairie it is today. In this rendering, it would have been known as Alachua Lake.
(Courtesy Florida State Photographic Archives)

a lot of "hatchees" are rivers, and "chobees" are water. You'll get the hang of it as we go along.)

There were no such people as Seminoles (a Creek/Cherokee name meaning "Wild Ones") until the infamous "Trail of Tears," when all tribes were forced to walk westward across the southern tier of states into the Oklahoma Territory, where they'd been "given" a new home. Those who escaped this heartbreak fled southward into Florida; they were the "leftovers," "remnants," and indeed Wild Ones, as our Cherokee consultant, Kenneth Moore, tells us, depending on which combination of dialects is used.

Every American schoolchild learns that the longest state of hostilities in man's history is the Hundred Years War between England and France. But the state of hostilities between the United States and the Seminole Nation extended from skirmishes in the 1820s, to cessation of action on August 14, 1842, to the actual treaty signing between the two nations in—1976! This was 134 years after the battles, with the U.S. government providing payment to each citizen of the Seminole Nation.

We think by now the reader can appreciate the prominence of Indian names in our state. Inspired by the storytelling nature of these Indian names, our earliest Crackers then began to experiment with name-giving ideas of their own.

Various syndromes seemed to infect the name-givers. We've chosen to explore here only a couple that reached epidemic proportions.

First among the ailments was "acronymitis."

The king of acronyms was probably the legendary Arthur Vining Davis, who came to Florida at the tender age of eighty-one! That's right. That's when he *got* here. He brought $300 million with him, too. He already had one major acronym under his belt, a little item he called "ALCOA"—Aluminum Company of America—which bore his imprimatur as a founder and leader. Within a short while, Davis, buying everything not nailed down, had created one of the giants of Florida industry, using the first two letters of each of his own three names. The result? Arvida. See, you're getting it. More on Davis in the "Empire Builders" chapter.

Among the towns to fall to the acronym hammer is Nalcrest, founded by members of the National Association of

Letter Carriers. Then there is Sumica, also in Polk County, developed by the Société Universelle Mining Industrie, Commerce et Agriculture, the French mining company that developed the land.

And don't forget the crossroads town of Kiko, named for the Kissimmee Island Cattle Company. (Or is it Kico . . . or Kicc?)

Though no acronym is involved, every citizen in Two Egg in Jackson County can tell you of the town's origin: A) Two brothers started a store. A guy came in and asked for two eggs. The brothers thought it sounded like a good name for a town. . . . Or B) Two brothers started a store. A little girl came in and said, "Ma wants one egg worth of bladder snuff and one egg worth of ball potash. . . ." (Pays your money, etc.) It's still a great name. Ask anybody in Two Egg.

Some would-be acronyms simply became contractions. For example, Albert T. Repp builds his 1920s land-boom hotel in the oceanside village of Delray Beach and wants some kind of immortality. We can't blame him for that. So he names his charming hotel the Alterep Hotel. It opens in March 1926 and closes in December 1926. It is the wrong end of the Florida land boom! (But the hotel is acquired by the Boughton family and becomes the delightful Colony Hotel, which is still going strong at this writing.)

Volco is a happy amalgam of Volusia and County. Manasota is a blend of Manatee and Sarasota. Now that's real syllable efficiency. So is Wayland, from two towns—Waycross and Lakeland—termini of a long-ago railroad.

Some contractions are harmless enough, as Bertha Bloodworth and Alton Morris have shared with us. Guess where Okeelanta is. Somewhere between Okeechobee and the Atlantic Ocean. Sanlando is somewhere between Sanford and Orlando. Gosh, it all seems so clear, now that we really can talk about it, and bring it out in the open. We don't want to squelch these things.

"Kanfla" is a contraction of Kansas and Florida. Guess where those folks came from? Or the town of Wiscon . . . it's pretty clear where their hometown was, too.

The award for "Best Name Tied to Local Industry" goes to (may we have the envelope, please) Phosmico, in Polk County, founded by Phosphate Mining Company.

A "Pure Imagination Award" should go to the folks over at Flomich! A happy combination of settlers named their town for Florida and Michigan. (We wonder if their putting Florida first had any special meaning. Naaahhh . . . probably just that Michfla would have been harder to pronounce.)

And the grandest award of all should probably go to the intrepid settlers working in the phosphate and limestone industries in the Marion County/Ocala region who came up with the Town Name to End All Town Names (next to Two Egg, of course). They called their town "Phoslime, City of Beautiful Homes."

THE "BACKWARDS-SPELLING TOOTH FAIRY" STRIKES AGAIN

And finally, we come to the famed "Backwards-Spelling Tooth Fairy" or old BSTF, as we'll call him. (Bad fairies are always a "him." Good fairies are a "her.")

He would strike where least expected, infecting some otherwise clear-thinking entrepreneur just as he was completing a million-dollar dream, and the poor victim would come up with the strangest-sounding monikers. Remember the Edsel? Well, that's sort of the way it works.

Try the town of Nolem. Folks built the town around the local melon market. They figured the town's gonna prosper from melons, so let's name the old place Melon. Naaahhh, let's give it some pizazz. Let's spell it backwards. Presto: Nolem. Presto #2: gone.

Or how about those Palmer folks from Chicago? They started their town on the Gulf and called the place—you guessed it—Remlap! Whatever happened to Remlap?

Then there was Mr. Haynes. He moved here, bought a bunch of acres to start his own town, and called it Senyah! Old BSTF strikes again.

How about that town down by the lake? Folks named it Lake. But it needed some pizazz, so they changed the name to . . . you're getting it . . . Ekal!

Some folks from an island off Georgia named Ossabaw Island named their Florida town Wabasso. And those folks from Arden, up in Pennsylvania . . . you got it. They named their Florida town Nedra.

To be fair, Old BSTF has infected humans for years. Remember the old Serutan tonic? Or how about the Camel Caravan program with Vaughn Monroe singing, "You're a Lemac Now."

A fine builder in Boynton Beach developed a whole section of Deriter Homes. It took us years to find out it was "retired" spelled backwards. But of all the BSTF giants of industry, the king of them all *has* to be (and you Crackers knew we were leading up to something) old "Handsome Jack." His story lies just ahead.

THE LEGEND OF OLD HANDSOME JACK

Old Handsome Jack; suave, dapper, gentleman-promoter, golfer . . . married to a DuPont heiress who would discreetly roll down her stocking and peel off enough $10,000 bills to seal a $70,000 deal—in cash.

Way to go, Handsome Jack!

Ol' Handsome Jack came to St. Pete smack-dab in the middle of the Florida land boom, the boom that would dwarf all the gold rushes put together, and all within one wild decade.

He brought together vision and money, drive and money, imagination and money, to create one of the grandest land-boom resort hotels of them all in St. Petersburg. It featured magnificent grounds, fountains, arbors, walkways, minarets, parapets . . . everything you could jam into a Florida land-boom resort hotel.

His dream hotel opened January 1, 1926, just at the edge of the incredible land boom . . . the rear edge. St. Petersburg historian and storyteller Ray Arsenault tells of the opening as if he had been there himself. Spotlights! Celebrities! VIPs! All the town's finest simply had to be at the opening. It was a dream world come true for Handsome Jack and his lovely wife.

The hotel closed in bankruptcy in the fall of 1927, less than two years after opening.

As Arsenault relates, Handsome Jack and his missus quietly slipped out of town, without their private railroad car, without their "his and hers" limousines, largely without funds.

And without being observed by hordes of creditors.

The deserted hotel lay fallow for some seasons, as Florida reeled from its incredible land boom and bust. It reopened years later as home of the Florida Military Academy, and still later as the Stetson University School of Law.

While the school makes knowledge of this history almost mandatory among present-day students, some alumni may learn here, for the first time, the history of their handsome campus buildings.

The Backwards-Spelling Tooth Fairy had struck again!

Handsome Jack's full name was Jack Taylor. The name of his dream hotel: The Rolyat!

THE ABCs OF PLACE NAMES

We've visited our original Indian-Crackers who left such a rich legacy in their language and names. We've checked out old Backwards-Spelling Tooth Fairy. Now it's time for some real place names.

With thousands of such names, it would be impossible to note them all. And with 58,000 square miles, over 7,000 lakes, 200 natural springs, and nearly 300 forts, camps, and posts, the project would be daunting. We won't even try to accomplish it.

But we will take you through your first "Florida ABCs," about some real Florida places. Later, we'll get to the ABCs of people, for it is people who make anyplace someplace.

We'll give you the first letter of the place name plus a clue or two. The little dash-lines will tell you how many letters and words there are in the name, and you take it from there.

You really should know most of these, but we don't have many fabulous prizes. (We don't have any prizes at all, come to think of it.)

For real Cracker children (you know who you are), it'll be a matter of pride. The rest of you just try to keep up as best you can . . . and no fair reading ahead in pages 26 through 35 to get the answers. (Those aren't the right pages anyhow. We just wanted to throw you off.)

Anyway, you'll get most of these, unless one of your tars is still in the sand and most of your jelly done fell off your cracker.

A is for A _ _ _ _ _ _ _ _ : Original name of Lake City. A toughie, unless your name is Goodbread, or maybe TV's Pat Sumerall, who is also a Goodbread. As is the author.

B is for B _ _ _ _ _ _ _ _ : Second grand hotel by Henry Plant after his Tampa Bay Hotel. A scenic, gabled wonder very much a treasure today.

B is for B _ _ _ : Simply means mouth. We have several: Grande, Raton, Ciega. *Grande* means big. *Ciega* means blind. *Ratón* means (sorry Raton) mouse.

C is for C _ _ _ _ _ _ _ _ : Very well known cape named by Ponce, meaning Place of Grassy Reeds.

C is for C _ _ _ _ _ _ : Famed island where the swashbuckling pirate Gasparilla kept his wives captive. Name the island, but don't be too sure about whether he buckled a swash or not.

C is for C _ _ _ _ _ _ _ _ _ : deNarvaez landed here about forty years before the settlement of St. Augustine. When this town broke away from Hillsborough County, it was decided that the first town to build a courthouse in the new county would be the county seat. Folks in this town secretly worked all night building a courthouse. The next morning, they were the county seat, and still are.

D is for D _ _ _ _ _ _ _ _ K _ _ : President Teddy Roosevelt caught a giant devilfish, a thirty-foot-wide manta ray, here. Weighed two tons (the fish, not T.R.). They named the place after him (also the fish, not T.R.).

D is for D _ _ _ _ 'S M _ _ _ _ _ _ _ _ _ : Gainesville's giant, funnel-shaped sinkhole, 500 feet across. When Florida's underground rivers drop to a new level, surface land follows suit, making instant Florida sinkholes. This one is one of her best.

D is for D _ _ _ _ _ _ City: This one's a toughie. A forgotten visionary who saw too far into the future and died too soon developed this tiny town near St. Petersburg. On his death, the name was changed to Gulfport. It is also the name of a great junior high school.

E is for E＿ ＿ ＿ ＿ ＿ Island: We live inside the universe, said Dr. Cyrus Teed and his Koreshan Unity Group. They settled this delightful beach island near Ft. Myers.

E is for the E＿ ＿ ＿ ＿ ＿ ＿ ＿ ＿ ＿: River of Grass. We'll just give you this one. Mr. "D" (go back two letters) said he was going to drain this sucker . . . about 2.5 million acres or so.

F is for F＿ ＿ ＿ ＿ ＿ ＿ ＿ ＿ ＿ Beach: While folks differ, this is probably the second oldest settlement on the continent. Florida has all six of the oldest.

F is for Ft. C＿ ＿ ＿ ＿ ＿ ＿ ＿ ＿: Probably the third oldest settlement. It got wiped out by the fourth-oldest group.

G is for G＿ ＿ ＿ ＿ ＿ ＿ ＿ ＿ ＿ ＿: de Soto marched through here in 1539! He called it Potano Province; Indians called it Alachua; farmers called it Hogtown. It had a whole bunch of names. It has Gators now.

G is for G＿ ＿ ＿: Palm Beach County exclusive enclave founded in 1950s by some gentlemen from Illinois, who simply liked to play the game. Name of their Illinois town, also.

G is for G＿ ＿ ＿ ＿ C＿ ＿ ＿ Springs: This town had four "angels," Hoover, Penney, Borden, and Grover Cleveland.

H is for H＿ ＿ ＿ ＿ ＿ ＿ ＿ ＿-by-the-Sea; Joseph Young's dream town and 1920s resort hotel. Fleets of busses brought buyers in from all over the Midwest.

H is for H＿ ＿ ＿ ＿ ＿ ＿ ＿ ＿ Springs: Seminoles liked it here and helped settle it in 1836. It spurts 70,000 gallons per minute. And this is a little one.

I is for I＿ ＿ ＿ ＿ ＿ ＿ ＿ ＿ ＿: In the Keys. Means Purple Island in Spanish. Pirates could navigate by miles of purple bougainvillea glowing on the horizon.

J is for J＿ ＿ ＿ Beach: Was county seat for entire Dade County, from the Keys to the Palm Beaches. Had a tiny railroad running from here to Jupiter, Venus, and Mars called— what else?—Celestial Railroad.

K is for K＿ ＿ L＿ ＿ ＿ ＿: Originally called Rock Harbour in the Keys, but the name was changed to match the Bogart movie about a hurricane with gangsters and stuff.

K is for K＿ ＿ W＿ ＿ ＿: Southernmost point in the U.S.

We'll just give you this one. Originally Cayo Huesos—Isle of Bones.

K is for K _ _ _ _ _ _ _ _ _: Town that Mr. "D" did help develop on that land he said he would drain in that famous swamp. Now home of the most famous tourist destination on Earth.

L is for L _ _ _ C _ _ _: Originally called Alligator. Home of Florida Sports Hall of Fame. If you have trouble with this one, go back to letter *A* and see if that helps you any.

M is for M _ _ _ _ _ _ _: Named for oranges; home of Harriet Beecher Stowe. It was said riverboat captains paid her to sit on her own front porch while they steamed by, so they could tell their passengers she was writing *Uncle Tom's Cabin*.

M is for M _ _ _ _ _: Named for Civil War governor who took his own life. Originally called Scratchankle and Hardscrabble. No one seems to know why.

N is for N _ _ B _ _ _ _ _ _: Was called Ormond both before and after it bore this name. Settled by folks from Connecticut and named after their Northern town.

O is for O _ _ _ _ _ _: World's smallest post office, in Collier County. The building is seven feet by eight feet. The postmistress had to step outside to change her mind.

P is for P _ _ _ _ _ _: St. Johns River lumber town. Has had the most names of any Florida town: Buena Vista, Gray's Place, Bush Post, Ft. Shannon, and finally this name. Has famous Ravine Gardens State Park. Incredible.

P is for P _ _ _-a-G _ _ _ _ _ Beach: The only place named after a charcoal grill. Fishermen stopped here to grill their catch.

P is for P _ _ _ _ _ _ _ _: Tristan de Luna established a colony here in 1559. They tried to "stick it out" three times.

P is for P _ _ _ _ R _ _ _ _: Means Flat Point. Tiny village near Ft. Myers. The first cable news of the sinking of the battleship *Maine*, leading to the Spanish-American War, was received here.

Q is for Q _ _ _ _ _: Town in Gadsden County named for a president's middle name, as are other towns in the North. (Many Florida folks remember the North.)

R is for R _ _ _ _ _ _ Beach: Hometown of Burt Reynolds, and one of the few towns in the Palm Beaches without the word *Palm* in its name.

S is for S _ . A _ _ _ _ _ _ _ _ _ : Once and for all, the oldest continuously occupied site on the continent (fourth settlement in Florida [1565], following Pensacola, 1559; Fernandina, 1560; and Ft. Caroline, 1562). A great place of pure history.

S is for S _ . C _ _ _ _ : The other town built on that drained swampland. Originally, a retirement town for Union Army Civil War veterans!

S is for S _ . P _ _ _ _ _ _ _ _ _ _ : Named by Peter Demens for his hometown in Russia. Also named by the American Medical Association as "The Healthiest Spot on Earth," the Sunshine City.

T is for T _ _ _ _ _ _ Trail: When this road name was announced, as a contraction of Tampa/Miami, critics asked, "Why don't we call the Jacksonville-Miami road the Jackiyami Joypath?" Really.

T is for T _ _ _ _ _ _ _ _ : In the Keys. A newsman said an enterprising saloonkeeper put up a poorly spelled sign saying *Tavernnier* pointing to his bar. Folks just kept the name, but spelled it right. We'll give you this one.

T is for T _ _ _ _ _ _ _ Island: St. Pete realtors boosted sales by spreading rumors of buried treasure here. But there was no treasure, and it went bust.

T is for T _ _ E _ _ : U.S. 90 in Jackson County. Two brothers opened a store. The first customer asked for this merchandise. They named the town after the customer's request. It makes a good story, anyhow.

U is for U _ _ _ _ _ : Probably the last development to "go bust" in the land boom in Miami. Named for the place where everything is perfect, but it didn't work.

V is for V _ _ _ _ _ _ _ _ _ _ : Dr. John Perrine named this after his Indiana hometown.

W is for W _ _ _ _ _ : Just like *V*, folks came from Wisconsin and named this place after their Wisconsin town. They make great TV commercials, too.

W is for W _ _ _ P _ _ _ Beach: Started as a shelter for workers building Henry Flagler's Dream City, across the lake. Workers rowed to work each morning and rowed back at night. That was some commute.

Y is for Y _ _ _ _ _ _ _ _ _ _ : Levy County Judge Knotts of Gary, Indiana first called the town Knotts, after himself. A lot of Yankees came down, so he changed it to this name.

Z is for Z _ _ _ _ Springs: There are a lot of sulphur springs in this area. Italian rail workers used this word for sulphur, and it became the name of the town. A time-capsule hamlet, like many all over Florida.

So there you have your Florida ABCs of places. Later, we'll cover ABCs of people, happenings, things, and stuff. (We know these are very technical terms, but this is serious business.)

We wish to express our deepest gratitude to historians Alton Morris and Bertha Bloodworth for their great research in *Places in the Sun,* from the University of Florida Press; to our legislative historian, Allen Morris; Joan Morris and Jody Norman, both stalwarts in the Florida State Photographic Archives; and our state Department of Commerce and Dixie Lee Nims. Without their help and resources, such data could never be assembled.

Gathering such material requires many specialists, from our ghost-town chronicler, James Warnke, to our St. Petersburg historian, Ray Arsenault, to Broward authority and storyteller Stuart McIver, to Tampa Bay expert Gene Burnett, to old friend Hampton Dunn. While credit to these persons and others appears elsewhere in these pages, a special nod is called for here to recognize the unique nature of our Florida "history tour" . . . and the personal stamp of each of these masters.

There will be other countless Florida sources to be recognized, from eminent historian Judge Jim Knott in the Palm Beaches, to Virginia Parks in Pensacola, to our friendly Yankee trivia experts, Ernie and Jill Couch and their "Florida Trivia" books from Rutledge Hill Press in Tennessee (well, maybe just barely Yankee), to Nixon Smiley, who was of great help in this section before he left us.

They're all great folk. Just thought you ought to know.

Our ABCs of places really weren't that tough, now were they? We didn't think one of your tars was still in the sand. You want the answers? They're comin' right up.

THE GOOD OLD DAYS WERE PROBABLY WHEN YOU WERE NEITHER

Now, let's check out some answers. Many of the names you probably knew, but then, you always did test well.

First, with the *A*, you should know by now that Alligator was the original name of Lake City. Under *A* we could have talked about Archer, founded by Quakers from Indiana, or Aripeka, near Tarpon Springs, an old Indian name meaning "A Pile at the Base," but that means a pile of scalps at the base of their warpole and we didn't want to upset you.

For the first *B*, Henry Plant's second grand hotel was the *Belleview* Biltmore.

Surely you got Boca, for Grande, Ciega, and Raton. At one point, scholars in the latter town actually set out to prove *Ratón* did not mean mouse.

We could have included Brighton, founded by Jim Bright, partner with Glenn Curtiss in Curtiss-Wright Aircraft. Curtiss founded Hialeah.

The first *C* word was Canaveral. The second was Captiva, where that swashbuckler Gasparilla held his wives. There *is* a Captiva . . . we're not too sure about Gasparilla.

You probably got Clearwater. We could have thrown in entries for Chipley, the "other railroader," or even Coral Gables, but we'll save those places for later.

And talk about some "gimme's," how about Devilfish Key? We even told you what ol' T.R. caught . . . but a toughie was Devil's Millhopper, the giant sinkhole in Gainesville. Disston City, named for Hamilton Disston, is now Gulfport, but Disston Junior High remains. Many wonderful people attended there.

Of course, for *E*, you got the Everglades, but how about Estero Island, where the Koreshan movement started?

Under *F*, Fernandina Beach is the second oldest settlement. The other *F* was Ft. Caroline, which became Jacksonville . . . eventually.

Under *G,* old Hogtown became Gainesville. The next answer is Golf, the Village of Golf, founded by that group of players from Illinois. The last *G* is Green Cove Springs, with those four "angels" to promote the little town and its springs.

Under *H* we have Hollywood-by-the-Sea along with Homosassa Springs, a favorite spot of the Seminoles.

I is for Islamorada, the purple island in the Keys.

Under *J,* Dade County once covered the entire region from Key West to Jupiter, and the county seat was the tiny town of Juno Beach.

Then a couple gimme's: Bogart's movie was, of course, *Key Largo*; Key West is the southernmost point in the U.S.; and Kissimmee is the town resting on land drained by Mr. Disston.

Under *L* we gave you a reverse reference, so you should have gotten Lake City, which was also Alligator, under *A.*

There are another couple of goodies under *M*: Mandarin was the tiny settlement favored by Harriet Beecher Stowe, and Milton, named for Florida's Civil War governor, was also called Scratchankle and Hardscrabble.

That early name for Ormond Beach was New Britain, where the folks came from in Connecticut.

The tiniest post office is in the even tinier town of Ochopee.

The first *P* is for grand old Palatka, where you find the incredible Ravine Gardens State Park. A "must-see." The place named for a cookout, of all things, is Pass-a-Grille Beach. Many Passagrilleans may learn for the first time the origin of their name. Originally called Passe-aux-Grilleurs, this was where fishermen would stop and cook their catch. They still do. The next *P* is Pensacola. Its settlement in 1559 was the beginning of the whole thing.

We could have given you a gully washer under *P*—Perrine, Plant City, Port Orange, and even Port St. Joe—but they'll all come up later, so we jumped to Punta Rassa. And you probably spotted Riviera Beach, hometown of Burt Reynolds in Palm Beach County.

Q is for Quincy, of course.

The oldest permanently settled site on the continent is St. Augustine. Menendez established a fort here in 1565. The other areas, they say, "just didn't stick it out." He also set up

All Florida cities began with packed, sandy streets and usually beam-timber curbs, eventually leading to gravel and finally paving, often by red or gray brick. This 1900 view of Central Avenue in St. Petersburg looks east to the bay, with the original Detroit Hotel tower in the far left. (Courtesy Florida Department of Commerce/Tourism Division)

As towns grew settled, natural charm grew as well; this was Atlantic Avenue in Delray Beach, circa 1930s, which led toward the camera, over the old wooden Intracoastal bridge, to reach Delray's ocean beach, a few hundred yards farther behind the picture-taker. (Courtesy Delray Beach Historical Society)

tiny missions in the areas of today's Miami Beach and Ft. My-ers. He left four priests at the latter, all named Gaspar. (Watch for these guys later.)

The *S* list also includes St. Cloud, on swampland drained by Disston, and St. Petersburg.

The *T* list includes Tamiami Trail, Tavernier, Treasure Is-land, and our legendary Two Egg, Florida.

U is for Utopia, where everything would be perfect, but this development got here just in time for the final curtain of the land boom. *V* is for Valparaiso. Under *W* we have Wausau, and West Palm Beach, currently smack-dab in the middle of America's number-one growth market.

Y is for Yankeetown. And finally *Z* is for Zolfo, the Italian word for sulphur. The tiny town settled by Italian rail workers became Zolfo Springs.

In a tour like this, we hated to miss the charm of Winter Park; the Gulf-side "feel" of Venice; "Delray Beach-by-the-Ocean" and "Naples-on-the-Gulf," just as the Sunshine City was once promoted as "St. Petersburg-by-the-Gulf-Stream" . . . but we'll meet all these and more, up ahead.

You've done very well under this incredible stress and pres-sure. We've only scratched the surface of the thousand place names, 7,000 lakes, and 300 military forts and posts. Our spe-cial thanks again to all those folks listed at the end of the quiz part.

THE LAST WORD ON PLACE NAMES

It was during the original Spanish occupation of Florida that the oldest British name began to appear, that of Jonathan Dickinson. In 1696, Dickinson, leading a group of Quakers from Pennsylvania, was shipwrecked in the Atlantic, offshore present-day Stuart on Florida's southeast coast. The group was actually escorted by Indians up the entire Eastern seaboard wilderness, back to Philadelphia, unharmed. Re-member, this was 1696! This is the only known instance of this sort. Jonathan Dickinson State Park, on U.S. 1 between Jupiter and Stuart, commemorates his name and the event.

When the British took over Florida in 1763, English names began to appear. Amelia Island honors Princess Amelia, daughter of King George III. Port Charlotte honors the wife of King George I, although Spanish historians say it could have derived from Carlos, i.e., King Charles, and be of French or Spanish origin.

Ponce de Leon named Cape Canaveral in 1513. Some 450 years later, six days after the assassination of President Kennedy, the Johnson administration agreed to rename the site Cape Kennedy. The American Society of Names pointed out that it had taken only thirty minutes to wipe out a place name that had been in existence for over 400 years . . . and one of the two oldest on the continent.

A compromise prevailed with the resulting name becoming the Kennedy Space Center at Cape Canaveral. One of the first names on the continent should not be so easily cast aside.

The Cape, from the air, appears to be the most perfectly designed spot on Earth for its role, a rocket base for outer space. It has not one, but *two* natural water barriers separating it from the mainland, and its landform comes to a natural point, jutting into the ocean. It even overlooks a 20,000-mile down-range tracking space called the Atlantic Ocean. Great planning by that Land Creator.

The town and county names in Florida salute over one hundred of America's "mighty": Flagler, Plant, Olds, Collier. Faraway lands are also commemorated. Yamato, between Delray Beach and Boca Raton, is simply an ancient name meaning "Old Japan." Creatures have been acknowledged (Alligator, Mosquito, even Bullfrog) as well as the climate (Belleair) and the plants (Live Oak).

Even the Suwannee River draws on history. Its name is said to derive from an early mix of Spanish, Indian, and African dialects in the pronunciation of "St. Juanee," meaning simply "Little St. Johns" as opposed to its neighboring giant.

In the Keys, one story tells of two rail workers pausing, with one commenting, "Boy, this job is getting to be a real marathon," so they named the place Marathon. (And if you'll buy that story, we have some land in the swamp we want to talk with you about.)

In the Panhandle (West Florida to Florida depression kids), the town of Marianna combines the names of Mary and Anna, members of the founding families. It's also where you find Florida's incredible Caverns State Park, Chipola River, Natural Bridge, and sites of two of Florida's Civil War battles.

Anglophiles who enjoy stories of London's ancient and polluted Fleet River, running (and sealed) beneath the venerated traditions of Fleet Street, may also trace the story of the ancient waterfall in the center of Old Tallahassee, called The Cascades. One day in the 1880s, a young lady walked into the falls and was drowned. Townsfolk decided to fill in the falls so such a tragedy might never happen again.

They were able to stop the falls, but not the source. The water is said to be still flowing, under Tallahassee, and is known as the Old St. Augustine Branch.

Tallahassee was chosen as the site of the state capital simply because it was about midway between the two capitals of the then-British Floridas, St. Augustine and Pensacola. A courier on horseback was sent from each capital with the agreement that, wherever they met, that spot would become the site of the new capital. The daughter of the territorial secretary was said to be allowed to suggest a new name for the site.

So now you know the answer to that eternal question, "How on Earth did your capital get way up there in the north, 400 miles from Miami?"

Down the road a piece, St. Joseph, where the original State Constitution was signed in 1838, had become, then, a booming, waterfront, resort town, with docks, tall ships, theaters, and hotels. It was expected to become the state capital in time.

It was also a bawdy town of brothels, cheap flophouses, and bars, all contrary to its biblical name. In 1841, events viewed by many as pure biblical retribution for its sinful ways occurred. First a yellow fever epidemic decimated the town's population. Many survivors simply fled. On their return, a major hurricane in 1841 almost leveled what was left of biblical St. Joseph.

Generations later, Ed Ball and the DuPont interests, developing the St. Joe Paper Company, secularized the name to Port St. Joe, and with this name, the town was reborn as a major paper industry port.

By the beginning of the 1990s, the Florida legislature was exploring a ten-year, $3 billion program, labeled as the most ambitious in the nation, to try and save her lands for future generations.

The bill, known as the "2000 Law," lets Florida lead the way in trying to protect her own environment for Cracker generations to come, to save precious terrain from being totally gobbled up as we hurtle toward our tomorrows.

As wise heads have agreed, there must be room for both Florida's major factions, developer/progressive interests on the one hand, and conservationist/naturalist concerns on the other. Any confrontational relationship cannot continue if Florida is to survive "healthy" through the coming century.

CHAPTER 2

The Water

WHERE DOES IT ALL COME FROM AND WHERE DOES IT ALL GO?

These pages will address Florida's water concerns—where it comes from, where it goes, and how much will be available tomorrow. The data derives from interviews with water officials, leaders, workers, and just plain folks, all of whom share the same concerns for this state's water. We will explore her rivers, lakes, marshlands, rainfall, and even her hurricanes.

Beginning on August 24, 1992, and continuing for nearly a week, a single event occurred that altered forever all records of Florida's rainfall, her storms, her storm damage, and even her traditional "hurricane memory." Hurricane Andrew hit dead center into one of the state's most densely populated areas, South Miami.

The megastorm affected nearly four hundred square miles of homes, buildings, and people. Its center wrapped so tightly that it spawned smaller tornadoes within itself, changing forever even our old-timers' grasp of what a Florida hurricane can do. It eventually wreaked an estimated twenty billion dollars in damage along the path of its 16.9-foot storm surge as it raced across South Florida.

Since much of a hurricane's power comes from its winds and its water, the Andrew disaster story will relate directly to these pages on Florida's water. However, an in-depth study of the state's hurricanes will await another time, another story, perhaps another book.

Florida's water concerns are vast and of great importance to the future of her 30 million Crackers-of-tomorrow. These pages do not attempt to be an engineering report, nor a scientific journal. Rather, they are an assimilation of hundreds of discussions with experts and "civilians" alike and a digestion of hundreds of reports, papers, and articles.

These pages will be only slightly scholarly, and totally in layman's terms so we may all try to understand better what our water experts are doing. We will also spotlight numerous questions directed at the author over twenty-five years of addressing countless groups of persons all over Florida; questions raised by Absolute Amateurs, to which our Absolute Experts often fail to provide Absolute Answers.

In virtually every Q&A session following an address, the very first question is, "What about our water?" Or, better put, *"What about our water!!!"* since it is usually asked with great vehemence, and most often shouted.

Through the 1980s and into the 1990s, the number of questions continued to grow, and only time will address some of the issues which arose: "Why has a 'Cross-Florida Canal' been the world's grandest political football for over two hundred years?" "Why did the Army Corps of Engineers dig 'The Big Ditch' and straighten out the winding Kissimmee River? Who told them to do it?" "Who's going to pay to clean up the mess?" "Why couldn't Florida have a canal system running the length of the state, connecting a whole bunch of lakes, ponds, and natural springs?" (We realize "bunch" is probably a technical term, but you get used to it. Besides, we really have to hunker down when we get to this subject.)

We'll paint some pictures of what Florida could be, with a beautiful trans-state canal system helping to create a unique Florida canal waterpark, bringing untold benefits to the state, and at the same time, delivering hundreds of millions of gallons of Florida's vanishing treasure, her water, from where there is much of it, to where it is desperately needed.

Since time began, man has centered his life around his water. His crude, reed huts; his teepees; his forts, castles, villages, and great cities all have been built near water. The cultures of China, India, Europe, Egypt with her "Mother Nile," and our own culture all focused on our universal need for water.

Florida is no exception to the rule.

Here, we will look at our total water picture: our water sources (where it comes from); our water usage (where it goes and how much we use); the struggles between Florida's two main camps, conservationists and developers; our dwindling supply; our weather; and future options.

One small-town legislator told the author, "Our water's probably OK, but someday we'll probably have to boil our *air* before we can breathe it."

During a period of severe air pollution in New York City, a city engineer was asked what he planned to do about the problem. He replied, "I plan to try not to breathe too much." His comment relates well to the often, semi-official posture among Florida leaders when the water problem comes up, which is just about all the time.

If we are to measure this posture from press releases to the media, Position Paper #1 will often say, "Well, you people out there just stop using so much water." Position Paper #2 might counter with, "Well, we'll just wait for the rainy season and everything will be all right."

With a thousand new Crackers arriving every day, Florida must turn to a plan that will transport some of her water from where it is, to where it is needed. It will be a plan that may work spectacularly well or it may work only very well. Or it may just work OK.

It simply cannot *not* work.

So let's take a look at Florida's water: where it is, how it gets there, and how we can get some of it back.

You've always wanted to know about aquifers? Well, here's your chance.

WHERE THE WATER IS

Florida's fresh water comes from three main sources: 1) Surface water, still and standing or flowing in ponds, lakes, and streams. 2) Underground water stored deep beneath the surface of the earth in aquifers. (We'll get to these in just a few moments. Coming soon to a page near you.) And 3) Rainfall, which really should need no introduction.

Underground water cannot really be measured. It lies in those aquifers we told you about; these are underground storage areas . . . spaces between layers of porous, sponge-like limestone. They literally store Florida's water for us. Our surface water slowly seeps down into an aquifer, seeking its own level.

By the way, 80 percent of all Florida's water comes from her aquifers, so it's a good name to know.

And by the way #2—if a break occurs in an underground rock layer, water there may plunge downward to a new level. Directly above this vacated space, surface soil instantly sinks to fill the void created by the water movement.

Result: another of Florida's famous sinkholes!

Florida's famous (or infamous) sinkholes have been known to devour roads, houses, cars, motor homes, boats, filling sta-tions, sidewalks, trikes, bikes, and buildings (not necessarily in that order).

They also create an instant, new tourist attraction; a large hole in the ground, filled with some or all of the above.

During the 1980s, several of these appeared. A major one in the Winter Park area gobbled quite a few of the aforemen-tioned items into a pit some 50 feet deep and about 350 feet across. Now, that's some digging.

Another major concern in our water-aquifer relationship is the danger of saltwater intrusion; i.e., when salt levels be-come so high in our fresh water supply, water in the area be-comes unsafe for residents to use, and pumping systems must be brought into the water plan to resolve the problem.

Surface water does not actually pour into aquifers. It seeps slowly down through the soil and layers of limestone, which absorb impurities as the water works its way downward three to four thousand feet below the surface, cleansing itself as it travels.

As it reaches its own level, water already there is forced out and up, into our water-pressure systems and into our lakes, ponds, springs, and wells in an eternal cycle.

Florida's natural wetlands are another link in our water chain. Our wetlands help store surface water, and help speed it downward into the aquifers. So wetlands play a vital and major role in the ecosystem.

When this delicate balance between surface water, wetlands, and aquifers is affected in any way, such as with the reduction of wetland areas, a major problem arises for Florida's water system of the future. By the 1990s, for example, a measurable portion of her historic wetlands had begun to disappear. Some of them were drained, some converted to pasture and farmland, and some covered with Florida's Official State Rock—gleaming white concrete—for Florida's continuous influx of new Crackers. (Yes, it was Will Rogers who said Florida began to change the day developers discovered that her sand was strong enough to hold a real-estate sign erect.)

The flow of concrete became so pronounced in the 1990s that a policy was developed calling for a "net-loss control" of wetlands. For every acre of pristine wetlands consumed by developers, another acre must be created.

It's a start.

AND WHERE IT GOES

The natural water ecosystem—water seeping slowly down into the aquifers, there building pressure, then rising into our pressure systems and surfacing in our lakes, ponds, streams, and swamps—has worked well for about fifty billion years or so, give or take a few billion years. (We told you this was not to be a scientific journal.) Anyway, this system has worked well for a long, long time, especially while Florida was experiencing *normal* (read old-fashioned) growth figures. How well it will carry us into the century just ahead is an entirely different story.

Florida's water problems in the 1990s and beyond loom ever more prominently:

Fact: Florida's water-starved Everglades continue to veer toward disaster with much of the water siphoned off to serve exploding coastal population.

Fact: It is estimated that up to one-half of all South Florida's water usage goes to her lawns.

Fact: Restrictions of some kind are probably here to stay. Half-hour daily sprinkling sessions will probably become a memory of yesteryear.

Fact: South Florida's water supply continues to dwindle. Experts predict continuing restrictions in the future, and these are based on the assumptions that the rains *will* come, and the problems *will* go away.

Fact: While restrictions may be here to stay, treated wastewater may provide respite; not for kitchens, but certainly for golf courses, parks, and estates. The Tampa area is already approaching this plan. Wastewater will be in use in many areas by the mid-1990s and, as many environmentalists say, only about twenty years behind schedule.

It is reasonable to assume that minds that can conjure up cities enclosed in giant bubbles floating in outer space, can surely devise systems that will provide clear, nourishing water here on Earth.

Fact: Desalination! Another magic word. And by the way, it's the same word as *desalinization*—except we save a lot of time by leaving out the extra *iz*. (We're thinking of you every minute.) Key West and Fort Pierce in South Florida already have desalination plans in action. Other plans are also in use on cruise ships sailing from Florida. More on that later.

Fact: Construction costs may climb as builders face impact fees and pass them along to consumers. Environmental rules will come into play more than in the past.

Fact: Cities will develop better systems for decorative water use, recirculating water for civic parks and city fountains, as with the beautiful lakes of Orlando and Lakeland.

Fact: By mid-1990, a new factor began to surface: *inter-county* water disputes. Miami's Dade County filed requests for water supplies to be drawn from underground reserves (these were those aquifers we told you about) and someone noticed the date on the forms was *twenty years in the future.* Neighboring counties protested, raising the specter of "water wars" in our Florida of tomorrow.

Fact: By mid-1990, Florida had experienced some thirty months or more of drought conditions. Lake Okeechobee, serving as both the "main" and "backup" source for South Florida water, was at a level of just under 10 feet—nearly 30 percent below normal for the lake. In 1981, it had reached its lowest level in history at 9.7 feet. Lock operators were asked *not* to operate the locks, which let boats move through the lake, since so much water is transferred during lock openings.

Fact: In spring of 1990, within one twenty-day period, enough water was taken from Lake Okeechobee to supply a city the size of Ft. Lauderdale for three full years. Remember, the lake was already at its lowest level in nearly a decade.

Welcome to the 1990s.

Fact: Florida's famed State Rock, her "concrete syndrome," actually has a major effect on her water ecosystem. As Florida converts more and more of her natural lands into burning, heat-reflecting ribbons of white concrete, she is actually changing the water cycle; i.e., rain falling to Earth is unable to become standing water which would then seep slowly down into the underground aquifers. Instead, the rain evaporates back into the atmosphere, having instantly vaporized upon hitting Florida's beautiful, gleaming, white concrete surfaces.

Fact: With records showing a dwindling of Florida's water, West Florida engineers have reported water supplies will have to grow by 2 to 8 percent per year over the coming decades to serve her "normal" growth rate.

Relate this to the reducing supply—the shrinking of the water supply by 3 to 5 percent per year over the past decade—and we can see the true dimension of the problem.

Fact: With Florida seeing about thirty-nine million visitors each year, with some thirty million folks visiting just one arena alone—the Central Florida "Themepark Belt"—with Florida now the fourth-largest state behind California, New York, and Texas, with about one thousand new Crackers moving to the state every day, and with up to twenty million residents expected by the year 2020, as the Old Cracker said, "That bridge we were gonna cross when we got to it . . . is here."

As long as we're checking facts, let's take a look at the weather.

Records show the decade of the 1980s to be Florida's hottest since 1870! Six of the ten hottest years in all Florida history occurred during the 1980s. The second single-hottest year in Florida history *ever* was 1989, and *it* was second only to 1988.

Apparently, when it comes to ozone-layer problems and

Earth-warming concerns, Florida has as good a head start as any place on Earth.

And you thought it was just the humidity.

It wouldn't be fair to leave our "facts" without checking in with some of our media and administration friends.

As if it were a real solution, our politicians and water czars sometimes adopt a uniform stance: "Tell the folks to quit using so much water."

And it works. They do.

In 1990, the town of Winter Haven came up with an historic "first." Following its own orders on water conservation, the townsfolk became so diligent in cutting back on water use that they found themselves facing a *new* shortage: money. The city had banked on budgeted funds, in part to be derived from projected water use. As usage plummeted, so did water revenues. The result was higher water bills.

SOUTH FLORIDA'S WATER SUPPLY

The key to South Florida's water is the aquifer system. Remember, *aquifer* simply means a space that holds water. (For you word experts, it has absolutely no connection to the word *aquifoliaceous.* Just thought you'd like to know. Aquifoliaceous actually refers to a member of the Florida holly plant, in case you're keeping track.)

But back to the aquifers. The entire Florida peninsula is a great, flat, sponge of very porous limestone, with a little soil and sand sprinkled over the top so folks can have lawns and cucumber farms, and raise sugarcane and maybe even some Aquifoliaceae around the place.

Now these underground limestone "pockets" are said to hold more water than in any other Eastern state. It is this water that rises to surface in our lakes, springs, and wells.

The second key must be giant Lake Okeechobee, our huge storage vault which contains so much of Florida's life-giving water treasure.

Fact: A change in Lake Okeechobee's water level of one-tenth of an inch—got that? one-tenth of an inch (either lowered or raised, but mostly lowered over the decade of the 1980s)—amounts to *eleven billion gallons of water* in the sprawling 770-square-mile lake. So we can imagine what a drop of four to five feet below its normal thirteen- to fourteen-foot depth can mean to the water supply of South Florida . . . and to the some six million Crackers in the neighborhood who rely on that water.

Fact: Even farther south, in the Florida Keys, a single, 130-mile pipeline carries some twelve million gallons of water *per day* down through the islands—their *only* supply. All of this means that water in the Keys can cost up to five times as much as on the mainland.

A unique experience is to be in the Keys on that rare occasion when a rupture occurs in the pipeline, as were the author and friends. A memorable Superbowl weekend was spent drawing water from the swimming pool to shave, shower, shampoo, sprinkle, and flush.

Nothing brings home the power of Florida water more powerfully than not having any.

THE PROBLEM OF GROWTH

Florida's water is logically (and irrevocably) linked to Florida's growth and, indeed, to her politics. As her leaders are occasionally reminded (at election time), any party claiming credit for the rainfall must remember that somebody has to take credit for the drought.

"Growth" is probably one of the most overworked words in the Florida lexicon, second only to two other words, "planned growth," and these two rank right alongside "controlled growth." The words are trumpeted at every turn by politicians, developers, and even, as Florida's eminent historian/author Hampton Dunn puts it, "by the whole dern *do-gooderin'* bunch."

Floridians are scolded by the day, hour, and minute, by economists and doomsayers alike. The headlines and sound bites become so familiar that they become, also, easily ignored by the listener/viewer/reader. They shout, "GROWTH MEANS BITING THE BULLET" (that's a good one), "FLORIDA GROWTH TO SLOW DOWN" (always an attention-getter), "FLORIDA HEADS FOR ECONOMIC SLOWDOWN," "FLORIDA GROWTH SLOWS DUE TO WATER SHORTAGE," and (one of the best) "FLORIDA MUST PAY FOR HER ECOLOGICAL SINS!"

The doomsayers get quite warmed up to their task with each new study, seminar, and/or weekend planning session. It appears the more expensive the plan and/or consultant, the more severe the warnings about Florida's countless ecological sins.

In 1990, then Governor Martinez, addressing a group of planners, remarked, "I almost hate to use the term 'growth,' since it seems to mean everything to everybody, but it narrows down to two basic needs for our population . . . our health care, and our *water!*"

Twenty-five years of travelling Florida and addressing countless Florida groups, panels, and seminars lead us to expand on the governor's syllogism just a wee bit. While growth is the single, underlying concern for our future, we can break it down into three issues: 1) Our population will be in the twenty million range well before the year 2020, and very possibly by the turn of the century. 2) Our very sustenance will be our water. 3) Growth means more waste to be disposed of.

At one seminar, an economist suggested that we should all devote our energies to combatting crime and poverty, since the seminar had predicted both of these to increase by 58 percent over the coming decade. The panel did, however, decide firmly that, where public apathy is concerned, folks mostly really don't care much one way or the other.

What is surprising, at least to thousands of good old Cracker-natives, is that the talk-show hosts and producers and the news editors and publishers seem to think that human nature can or will actually change. In the cold, hard light of common sense and street-smarts, there is no real indication that Florida's growth will suddenly, simply disappear . . . nor will it stop because of water, or any other of her growth problems. For example, there is no real indication that *people* (remember, that's our issue number one) will ever stop wanting to enjoy a delightful, warm climate in their maturing years. Nor will they ever stop looking to America's Sunbelt for a second home, cottage, or condo-by-the-sea.

One legislator, asked if he was indecisive in his position on Florida's growth, said, "Well, yes and no."

How can Florida be certain of some sort of a growth pattern through the coming three, four, or five decades? It's simple. Very few people ever retire to Chicago. Few really seek out a retirement spent ice-fishing in Duluth, or Green Bay, or in the Canadian North Woods. (You know who you are.) Now these are great places, but in plain old Cracker horse sense, none of Florida's charm and attractions are really going to just "go away." Florida can never legislate human nature, nor can she build a giant wall along her borders to keep everyone else out.

Florida will make mistakes. She will suffer from them. All her people will suffer from the greed and aggrandizement of the aggressive "takers."

And the "givers" will probably end up paying the bill in the end.

As our old Cracker parson in the little Corinth M.E. Church would say, "I want to be around when the meek inherit the earth . . . so I can watch the *un*meek take it away from them."

HISTORY ALWAYS REPEATS ITSELF, BUT EVERY TIME IT DOES, PRICES ARE ALWAYS HIGHER

We simply gotta have a plan.

While water plans will come and go, and will differ from one another, the simplest premise is that Florida will need, and must develop, a water network—a means of transporting her existing water from where it is to where it is needed.

Imagine a scenic, multipurpose network of modest canals, linking ponds, lakes, and springs together into a state-long waterpark, yet also transporting priceless water *down* the length of the state, letting the water seep into the aquifers as it slowly travels. It's a crazy idea, but it just might have a giant effect on Florida's water concerns for tomorrow.

But no matter what the plan, within the coming twenty to thirty years it will become imperative for Florida to have one in order to survive in her present state. And it does have some advantages over those other "plans" we heard about; you remember, Plan A—wait for the rainy season—and Plan B—you folks quit using so much water. These plans served us well for many centuries. How they will serve 30 million Crackers in the century ahead remains to be seen.

In another plan, of special interest to the sugar industry, a coalition of industry, business and naturalist groups suggested the state provide some three billion dollars to buy up 700,000 acres of sugar industry lands, flood the acreage, and create a giant water reservoir in a fifty-year program.

While such a plan may have merit, it would also wipe out thousands of jobs, cripple a major Florida industry (one which provides one-fifth of America's sugar crop), and yet still require the procurement of the water to fill the reservoir.

It was partly in response to this plan that an attorney for the sugar interests came up with the deep, thought-provoking comment that "it is actually quite possible that Florida's two main groups, environmentalists and developers, *can* co-exist, to have our ecology and our economy survive, side by side. . . ."

For some time, writer Michael Saunders produced a fine column for the *Sun-Sentinel* called "Water Whys." In various columns, Saunders reminded his readers that many years ago, a lot of South Florida interior land was under several inches of water much of the year, with the water provided and taken away by that timeless cycle of rain and drought, just as in ancient Egypt thousands of years ago.

Saunders also referred us to a reader, Miles Wood, who came up with a humdinger; an old, yellowed newspaper clipping containing a nugget of information that really should get serious consideration from water managers.

The "nugget" was simply a canal plan, which pointed out that: A) Florida has over seven thousand lakes and ponds, with over four thousand square miles of her land under some form of inland water. B) Florida has over two hundred natural springs—the highest concentration of these on Earth, and all within an area reaching from south-central Florida around to mid-Panhandle. The "shocker" is that these springs are spewing (and that's the only word for it), spewing forth some eight billion gallons of fresh, cold, pure spring water every single day and have been since time began (and probably even before that). In fact, Wakulla Springs is said to be the world's deepest, and one of the world's largest, along with Silver Springs near Ocala. These two alone account for nearly two billion gallons of water per day and have since time immemorial (or at least for a long, long time).

Early sightseeing boats at Silver Springs, the world's largest springs, were rowboats, each with a panel of thick glass built into the bottom. Almost a billion gallons of crystal-clear spring water bubble from underground chasms every day from Silver Springs alone, just one of over two hundred springs in Florida. Another billion comes from Wakulla Springs each day as well, the world's deepest. (Courtesy Silver Springs Photo Service)

"Well, where is it all going?" you query. (Thought you'd never ask.) Fortunately, we are storing all these eight billion gallons of water in two vast reservoirs, one just west of Florida, called the Gulf of Mexico, and one just east of town, called the Atlantic Ocean. Now, getting the water out of the reservoirs when we need it may pose some problems, but we'll cross that bridge when we get to it. Maybe the rainy season will come back.

Oh yes, many of these springs are actually owned by the state. And they've been producing that eight billion gallons of spring water every day for, oh about thirty or forty million years, so their permanency should not be too great a concern.

Now let's get on to item C and our actual plan. (Oh yes, one small note; those eight billion gallons every day are coming from just the fifty-one largest springs, and Florida owns about half of these.)

C) Why wouldn't it be possible to have a meandering, interconnected series of canals, aqueducts, streams, or even ditches, transporting even a little bit of the natural springs water from where there is so much of it to where it is badly needed? It's an astonishingly basic idea.

It is difficult to imagine any harmful impact that might be created by this gently flowing ribbon of cool water, drifting slowly from one lake or pond to another as it wanders down the spine of the state to its destination—the southernmost tip of Florida—then exits into the Gulf after having done immeasurable good along the way. If anything, the impact would be beneficial. It would create water hammocks, sloughs, and cooling reservoirs, and allow moisture to reach the aquifers.

However, as Saunders points out, the "aqueduct plan" surfaces every few years, and is usually met with some of those famous "mixed emotions," or is overwhelmed by objections to the idea.

A common objection is "the complexities of such a plan render it infeasible." Everyone seems to find different ways of saying, "We're in favor of that in theory, *but* . . ." (It is hard to imagine that engineers who bring us color TV from the far side of the moon will have trouble with a meandering series of large, attractive ditches.)

Another objection claims that "farmers would be sure to pitch a fight when it came to acquiring lands for such a network."

It is difficult to imagine any Florida farmer, looking over his parched acreage, finding any reason to fight a plan that might bring priceless water even near his lands.

Another objection refers to the division of water among farmers, city dwellers, and industry. Since the main purpose of the plan is to deliver more water, with already plentiful water to begin with, the issue of who was using the most would become a non-issue.

Wood writes that, according to the ancient newspaper article, "instead of letting our water from Florida's springs simply run off into the Gulf and Atlantic, we would let the canal plan transport even a little bit of the water to where it is badly needed. End result? Bringing water from Florida's central highlands into her parched South Florida flatlands, letting it seep and soak into the aquifers along its way."

If any group of Florida's springs could be connected by our chain of modest canals, diverting only a 1 to 2 percent "share" of our water, from any fifteen to twenty of Florida's already-owned springs, arithmetic quickly shows a flow of up to a quarter-billion gallons of water per day, slowly meandering down the spine of the state . . . eventually flowing into Lake Kissimmee.

"Why Lake Kissimmee?" you ask. Ahhh, that is the clincher. Because, from that point on, much of the canal was completed *about a hundred years ago*, by Hamilton Disston in his own personal dream of a Florida deep-sea, freighter-friendly canal system. Most often, the incredible objections raised each time the canal plan surfaces only reflect a lack of knowledge about this simple fact: almost one-half of such a system already exists.

Extending from Lakes Kissimmee and Tohopekaliga in Central Florida, and on lands he originally owned, Disston created his own chain of channels leading to the Kissimmee River, down to Lake Okeechobee, through more canals, into the Caloosahatchee River, out to Ft. Myers, and into the Gulf of Mexico. The system was dug to float Disston's freighters and to develop an interhemispheric shipping empire, all through a Florida canal system.

Disston's freighter channels actually became a water system without being planned for the purpose at all in one of the great serendipitous happenings of our age. Since necessity is the mother of invention, perhaps a canal park system will eventually come to be. In fact, it will have to.

The first hundred years are always the hardest.

THE OLD HAMILTON DISSTON SERENDIPITY TRICK

The Disston plan involved a chain of canals, a dozen or more lakes, and even the dream of a cross-state canal that, had Disston lived, would have reached eastward to the headwaters of the St. Johns River, thus opening the way to a vast north-south Florida water system . . . and offering solutions for which we would not be searching today.

As countless historians have pointed out, it is fascinating to imagine the effect had Disston's canal system been completed in the "simpler" time of the 1880s, and had he eventually run his waterways directly southward, through the wetlands of today's Everglades and into the Gulf, as well as westward to Ft. Myers. The effect on Florida's parched lands would have been extraordinary.

The Disston plan extended to today would nurture Florida's surface water. It could continually replenish giant Lake Okeechobee to the "full" mark, as well as provide backup water, and replenish the Everglades wetlands.

Disston used parts of the old, winding Kissimmee River in his system. It was 1948 when the Army Corps of Engineers began the famous "straightening of the Kissimmee," the project which, on completion, almost immediately began to wreak havoc on South Florida's natural water ecosystem. It was the 1990s before action was begun to try to undo the damage and restore the river to its original, meandering banks. The project is still underway at this writing. Restoring the river to her natural banks will be a small step toward providing a "water strainer" to cleanse her water as it flows slowly into Lake Okeechobee.

Even as the repairs to the Kissimmee are underway, Florida, under a new policy, has acquired over a million acres of

We are indebted to Judy Jacobsen for her spectacular photographic work of Florida's mightiest of rivers, the St. Johns. Here is evidence of the incredible effect a major river can have on the development of a city. (Photo by Judy Jacobsen Photographic Service, Jacksonville)

To try to view the Jacksonville city limits, Judy Jacobsen resorted to balloon shots—and still could not reach the city limits sign. The meandering St. Johns River finally reaches the Atlantic far into the distance, still in the city of Jacksonville. (Photo by Judy Jacobsen Photographic Service, Jacksonville)

water-sensitive lands in just seven years' time to try to protect and preserve her water resources.

And while this is not presumed to be an engineering study, and while today's engineers and consultants continue to say that a canal plan would be infeasible, probably several million Florida "civilians" gaze out over their beautiful, tawny-brown August lawns and say . . . "Why not?"

There are over two hundred natural springs in Florida. Any fifteen or twenty will do just fine.

OUR INCREDIBLE SHRINKING FLORIDA

As some wise philosopher once said, "We live in a world of contradictions. Then again, maybe we don't." Remember the old vaudeville one-liner . . . no, that was way before your time . . . about the hair restorer that didn't actually give you more hair, it would just shrink your skull so that the hair you *have* will cover it? Well, even the shrinking of Florida is not gonna solve all her problems in the coming century—least of all her disappearing water!

It's a fact; researchers have actually determined that Florida's east coast is slowly slipping into the Atlantic Ocean and her west coast is gradually losing several inches per year into the Gulf of Mexico, as well as into various man-made inlets along her coasts. Some surveys maintain that her eastern seaboard is actually disappearing by up to four inches per year, and her west coast by up to *one foot* per year!

Hard as all this may be to grasp in the present-day context, think of the ramifications when viewed through the telescope of, say, the next fifty to one hundred years. Faced with challenges such as these, homeowners and government alike will be investing millions of dollars to replenish sand on the beaches. We may even see sand wars between towns and neighborhoods over who is getting whose sand, to go along with those "water wars" we told you about.

Part of the loss is blamed on Florida's inlets—her openings through the barrier islands leading to the sea. Some studies even report that if it weren't for Florida's inlets, her beaches would actually be building up in places.

Scientists report that several factors play roles in the shrinking of Florida: A) The warming of the earth's atmosphere.

B) Build-up of heat-absorbing gasses over our water areas. And C) The resulting "greenhouse effect." All combine to create a possible rise in our sea level of two to twelve feet by the year 2100 (that's the bridge we were going to cross when we got to it).

While engineers indicate (and they're the guys on our side) that the two-foot estimate is probably the most likely, it is still only an estimate. As Will Rogers said, "An expert's guess is liable to be just about as good as anyone else's" (or maybe that was W. C. Fields).

However, the engineers got together with the math fellas, who had a slide rule (you remember slide rules) and came up with the fascinating fact that for each *one-foot* rise in our sea level, our shorelines can recede by *fifty feet or more.*

So now we have our Incredible Shrinking Florida.

No one wants to contemplate such a strange phenomenon as land simply disappearing into the sea, especially at such dimensions as these, but perhaps none of us at this moment will be around to worry about it. Remember, the best thing about the future is that it comes one day at a time.

Some engineers report (and maybe these guys weren't on our side) that a one- to two-foot increase in the level of our seas surrounding South Florida could result in the lower "toe" of the peninsula becoming an enormous, shallow, saltwater bay—with water perhaps six inches deep, covering the entire region from Tamiami Trail down through the Everglades, including all the Ten Thousand Islands area and Everglades City.

Some reports and research indicate the possibility of water actually covering the Keys in the coming century or so.

And as historians, articles, and works such as Robert McClure's fine South Florida Series in the *Sun-Sentinel* point out, to see the Florida of tomorrow, simply turn to the Florida of yesterday. If we go back in time, we find that the lower third of the peninsula actually was under water, the world's most fantastic river—about forty miles wide and six inches deep—Marjory Stoneman Douglas's famed River of Grass.

We call it the Everglades.

And so, we've taken you on a journey from ancient civilizations with their primal need for water, to our own leaders ordering the Army Corps of Engineers to "straighten the

Kissimmee with a big ditch" (the straightening was said to have created immense tracts of new, arable lands, but for *whom?*), and now into the 1990s, as Florida seeks to regain her birthright, her priceless water.

We've journeyed through the incredible Hamilton Disston dream of a Florida inland shipping empire, freighters, canals, and all! He is the man who envisioned the Florida waterpark canal system we will need tomorrow, but who did it over a hundred years ago.

Florida's media will play a role in changing her way of looking at her water concerns. In reviewing nearly two hundred articles and news-stories from 1989 and 1990, we find that certain prevalent themes continued to appear. In no particular order, they included: A) How you people can live with less water! B) How not to flush your toilet and not to water your lawn. C) How to landscape your yard with no grass. D) How come people "over there" are using more water than we are, and how bad is it going to be in the future. E) It's time to bite the ecological bullet and pay for our sins (or was it pay for our bullet and bite our sins?).

Now, a very simple approach, which was probably the way Hamilton Disston looked at things in the simpler time of the 1880s, might have been: A) Is there some water? B) Where is it? C) Can we get even a tiny little bit of it? D) Will it hurt anybody if we get it? E) How do we get it from where it is to where we need it? F) How much will it cost? G) Then let's get it.

Now, while such a plan is not nearly so grandiose nor headline-grabbing as a fifty-year plan costing $3 billion, part of its beauty is that it actually could be tried on a modest scale and continued as its effectiveness was measured and accounted for. If only one group were to start just one canal, from one small, state-owned spring into one nearby lake or pond, eventually leading into Lake Kissimmee, the plan would be underway.

Just ahead, we'll take you on a minicruise along the grandest political football of them all, the Great Cross-Florida Barge Canal. You'll have to come along, otherwise you probably won't believe the story. Stranger than fiction is Florida.

THE CANAL—BOONDOGGLE OR BUST!

Once upon a time, there was a great idea. It was called the Cross Florida Barge-Ship-Boat Scenic Canal, or something like that. It could have been a grand success for all Florida.

It would have moseyed slowly across the upper reaches of our magic land, not botherin' anybody, just carryin' little boats, people, hikers, picnickers, and campers along its route, as it wandered across North Florida's gently rolling lands. (Now, you folks in our great Northern big cities may have to look up *mosey*, but it's there . . . and believe me, this canal would have *moseyed!*)

Some of the folks, Thomas Jefferson, for one, thought it might be a pretty good idea. It appears that ol' Tom may have had a lot of foresight into Florida's water problems two centuries before the rest of the folks. (He was also probably one of the folks who said, "Remember, it wasn't raining when Noah built the ark.") And in the beginning, plans for a canal were worked on by—are you ready?—President Thomas Jefferson!

No, wait. Things started even before Tom, clear back to the 1560s. Menendez, after founding St. Augustine, figured there must be a better way to get around Florida, and felt it would be nice to have a little old canal across the neighborhood instead of having to sail a thousand miles or so down around the Keys to get into the Gulf. Anyway, the whole place was his, so he could do just about whatever he wanted. (They didn't even have any zoning laws or nothin', boy . . . and that committee meeting to study apathy was canceled for lack of interest). Besides, he had just sailed that route a couple seasons before, and he knew what a commute that was going to be in a few years. He even stopped off to visit Ft. Myers (of course, Ft. Myers hadn't been invented yet, so there really wasn't a whole heck of a lot going on).

The canal could have created a handsome, natural greenbelt, a scenic park—maybe a thousand yards wide or so—traversing the breadth of North Florida. Now, just imagine a pretty canal running down the center of the park, with a little roadway along each bank. Add picnic shelters and rest stops and you have some idea of what these fellas could have put together, way back when . . . and what still very well could happen in our future.

The canal could have been used for these past 400 years by canoes, rowboats, little fishing boats, or even no boats at all except in times of natural emergencies. The ideas can just roll on and on.

The incredible part is that there probably is no reason why the thing still couldn't work today, and certainly into the next century, and create an incredibly handsome attraction for the heartland of Florida for all her folks to enjoy.

By the 1990s, a few Florida legislators got the idea to try to create a cross-Florida park, using parts of the original lands planned for the original bunch of canals . . . the canals dating clear back to when old Tom Jefferson suggested we dig the thing.

This new plan would convert some 77,000 acres of land into state-owned parklands, stretching about 110 miles from Yankeetown, on the Gulf Coast, to the St. Johns River.

Since the canal question seems to arouse such intense feelings from so many sources every time it comes up, and if we really want to know where folks stand on the question, why not ask the folks in the neighborhood what they think of the idea? Would they like having a nice waterpark in their area, adding to the economic well-being of towns and businesses along the way?

That's just what the legislators began to do. And if this traditionally very conservative group were to find the plan attractive, think what the movers and shakers, the progressives, might have to say about the benefits of such a canal, especially since one-third or more of the parkland/canal dream is already finished, with locks and all, and has been working for a generation.

True. The encouraging and astonishing fact, as the assistant executive director of the Canal Authority of the State of Florida, Fred Ayer, reminds us, is that something more than one-third of the original 110-mile-long canal project is actually in use, and has been for years. Nothing beats good news, Fred.

The project is as old as the white man's awareness of this magic land. Menendez died thinking there must be a way across this new land by a water route. Within some 370 years after his death, by the time FDR was in the White House, there had been twenty-eight—count 'em—twenty-eight different surveys of the best routes across Florida by water.

And the good news is that a canal system has actually been successfully created in South Florida. A series of waterways and canals link parts of the region with vast Lake Okeechobee, enabling boaters to cross the state from the Jupiter area on the lower southeast coast, to Lake Okeechobee, and thence to the Gulf Coast at Ft. Myers via the Caloosahatchee River. Then, there is also Hamilton Disston's famous dream to consider (neither to be confused with the Ancient Football).

THE GRANDEST POLITICAL FOOTBALL OF THEM ALL

One of the most incredible parts of dealing with our grandest football etc. is finding so few people who even knew it ever existed, or almost existed. It is probably one of the least-explored, least-written-about giant projects in the land.

Let's just take it from the top and see what makes the canal such a front-running candidate for our grandest etc. award.

1820s—President Thomas Jefferson and his secretary of war view the canal as a good idea, especially if it creates advantage for U.S. merchant ships over Cuban shipping interests. Study is completed. Florida has only been part of the country (as a territory) for about twenty-four months.

1830s—"Funding" is invented. Federal Congress funds some $10,000 to complete studies for locks and canals. Submitted in 1832. Plan is met with mixed emotions, predominantly indifference. One congressman, asked if he knew the difference between ignorance and indifference, replied, "I don't know and I don't care." (Then again, maybe *that* was W. C. Fields.)

1850s—Civil War on horizon. Jefferson Davis initiates study on canal route with locks to end in Tampa Bay as warplan. Will cost grand total of $2 million to dig the whole thing, the cost of running today's federal government for about 2 1/2 minutes (excluding overtime and cost of studies and consultants). It would have been a heck of a bargain at the time, but what did we know? We'd only been Americans for about five years. Some of the stores hadn't even started their Washington's birthday sales yet.

1870s—Josiah T. Walls, Florida's famed black legislator, who served in the State House, in the State Senate, and in the U.S. Congress, urges study of a canal plan for Florida. This is met with more mixed emotions, as in the 1830s. Supporting the canal becomes tantamount to being named to the U.S. Olympic javelin team—as number-one catcher—or lifeboat drill instructor on the *Titanic*.

1909—Still another study by the Army Corps is ordered to determine a canal route. Met with similar mixed emotions.

1924—Still another study, for heaven's sake. For whatever reasons, again meets with mixed emotions. It was the land boom and everybody was too busy making money to be bothered with the deal. Besides, potatoes were cheaper, tomatoes were cheaper, and it was the Roaring Twenties!

1927—President Coolidge approves the deal! Incorporates twenty-eight different canal studies into one plan, and settles on the St. Johns/Oklawaha/Locks/Inglis route. Now, we're really gonna see some action, by gollies. Old Silent Cal is on the job!

1930—With the stock market crash, national depression, and Florida hurricanes, the project lies dormant. Folks just can't get it together. It now looms as a $100 million plan, a "barge-ship-boat canal" with high-level docks to "keep from scratching the aquifers," for heaven's sake. (Aquifers have been around for billions of years, and are about one to four thousand feet below the earth's surface. It's hard to see how a ten-foot ditch is going to scratch one, but that's what the fellow said.)

1930s—By this time, we've invented consultants, committees, and study advisors, so it's nellie-bar-the-door from now on.

1935—With New Deal funds, FDR now approves the project, and the action creates a genuine miniboom all along the proposed canal route. It creates a euphoria in the neighborhood. Some Jasper probably writes a hit song called, "Oh, There's Euphoria in the Neighborhood Tonight." Other areas of Florida now begin to react with those mixed emotions:

doubt, a little suspicion, some envy, and stir in a pinch of re-
sentment, as they begin to think the project may not really
benefit their neighborhood at all! They might not get in on
the Annual Euphoria Festival. This mix begins to reveal some
of the less-attractive parts of the old Cracker mind-set, i.e.,
"let's fight this thing at all costs!" (Since then the attitude has
gradually begun to lessen, but still remains a tiny, lurking
part of the Cracker mind-set; that someone else's dream
might cast a shadow over one's own region.)

This haunting philosophy/attitude surfaced again in the
1970s with the opening of the world's most famous tourist
destination, in the center of the state. Although it was hailed
by all Florida, businesspersons began to witness the demise of
tourism in South Florida, as fifteen to thirty million tourists
each year went to Central Florida instead of to their area. But
back to the old football. There's lots more.

That year FDR authorizes $5 million in relief-job funds,
saying the project will advance Florida development by 100
years! He authorizes a standing committee to study the
project. One committee member retires due to illness and fa-
tigue. Says he's sick and tired of the whole thing.

Ed Ball of DuPont interests says it will be the outstanding
accomplishment of the twentieth century and money must be
raised. Florida learns the trouble with money. It never comes
with a good instruction book, and even if it's a gift, it's usually
the wrong size. And besides, even though it's 1935 and potatoes are still cheaper, tomatoes are still cheaper, canals are
getting more expensive by the year.

1939—FDR appropriates $4 million more in canal funds.
Four thousand acres of land are cleared; 13 million yards of
dirt are moved. *Wow!* This thing is really gettin' goin'.

1940s—Genuine Florida depression kids will remember
huge "bridges to nowhere," straddling old 19, 441, and other
roads. These were giant bridge supports with no roads
hooked onto them. They were all part of the canal-to-be.
(Here you thought they were some ancient Florida Stone-
henge. Nope. They were part of Our Canal. And boy, we're
really gettin' underway!)

1940—Some three thousand students occupy barracks to
continue digging. Now it's a defense project. Don't you
know there's a war on? Somehow, Florida is not invaded and

luckily, we don't need our canal to evacuate the Atlantic seaboard. Whew!

1942—Another try by FDR. Now it's up to $40 million in projected defense funds, as a wartime security project. It still lies in limbo. There are probably more mixed emotions.

1956—Project surfaces again as a means to lower freight rates. This time, sponsors of the bill can't get it together. It's the 1950s and everything is cool, so don't rock the boat. Remember, we only had two rules. Rule #1 was don't sweat the small stuff. But Rule #2 was it's all small stuff. (It was a simpler time.)

1960—John F. Kennedy gives his pre-election blessing to the project, pledging funds to be set aside if he is elected.

1964—President Johnson urges work to get underway again. He provides an extra million to begin building a bridge in Palatka. Boy, now things are really gonna *roll!* He says the work will benefit the poor in small towns. You know, there's nothing bad about being poor except the poverty. Then President Johnson actually comes to Florida to look at the canal! This a first! He wishes the diggers well. Maybe he should have contacted the Gasparilla Treasure Diggers, Inc., of Sanibel and/or Captiva. We hear they've done very well. Maybe he doesn't know about them.

Then $4 million in canal funds are set aside for digging.

1965—Funds grow to $70 million.

1967—Now we're up to $76 million.

1968—Oops, we're back to $70 million.

1969—And back to the old $64 million.

1971—President Nixon, apparently determining this project to be too costly and poorly managed, orders all work stopped. One reporter says, "I guess we won't have the ol' Florida canal to kick around for another few hundred years," but nobody laughs.

1970s—By now, some fifty million dollars had been spent with only about one-third of the work completed.

1979—President Carter, determining it would cost only about fifteen million dollars to undo all the 160 years of work, requests authority to de-authorize the entire project. Florida's grand canal plan comes to a screeching halt.

Today, it would take in the neighborhood of two hundred

million dollars to accomplish what could have been done in the 1830s for about two million dollars.

It was, and still will be, a wonderful dream for Florida, and still will come to pass in our future. Its only victim thus far has been the public taxpayer, who has been paying for the entire dream on the 150-year installment plan since Thomas Jefferson's day.

A cross Florida canal would make the best use of the state's dwindling treasure, her water. The waterway could be connected to a series of canals, flowing down the peninsula, eventually connecting to the Kissimmee/Okeechobee waterway system created over a hundred years ago by Hamilton Disston. It could serve as part of a giant *"T*-formation" water system, with canals and waterways bringing water from Florida's midlands southward to her parched Everglades. This way, it is possible—just possible—that the Florida "water ogre of tomorrow" might be defanged.

In summation, such a canal-system could: A) Inject great benefits into the life-style of Florida. B) Provide a lift to the economics of the north-central region, through which the canal would travel. C) Contribute to a *T*-formation system of waterways that could deliver needed water to South Florida. D) Add to the scenic beauty of the already-proposed 110-mile-long "waterpark," "greenbelt," or now "Greenway Plan." E) Bring thousands of new visitors to Florida's heartland, visitors who would be seeking the state's natural beauty, wildlife, and parks. F) In such a dream canal plan, if use of boats were to be included, the project would create an entirely new traffic pattern for the boating world, as boating fans would head for these new cruising grounds, just as with the Chesapeake Bay, Long Island Sound, and other cruising areas. G) And a Florida canal system would add an entirely new dimension of charm and beauty to her inventory of attractions, ranking alongside the nation's intracoastal system but entirely within her own borders.

As Florida sees a thousand new Crackers arriving daily, she will have to find a place to put them, but also must enable them to shave, shower, shampoo, scrub, sprinkle, drink, dunk, and flush. And the one bottom-line certainty about water is that its concerns and problems recognize no boundaries.

Small towns, great cities, and rural areas are all touched by this issue.

Think about it. Southeast Florida residents use and consume some 1,500 gallons of water per person per day! Why is this pertinent to Florida's water concerns? This is fifteen times the national average consumption rate of 100 gallons per person.

Pinellas County, Florida's most densely populated area, reports underground water sources are severely depleted, with area wells showing possible contamination from overpumping for decades. Some water seems to have been pumped from *beneath the soil of neighboring counties* (shades of water wars). Similar problems may well develop in most of South Florida's heavily populated regions along with the greater Tampa Bay area.

In his probing book, *Sunshine States,* Patrick Carr has carefully researched many ecological concerns of the greater Tampa Bay area, including those about water, and the role of local government in planning for use and availability of that water. As Carr mentioned, "Remember, we may not be getting all the government we're paying for. For which, probably, we may all be thankful."

And among delightful stories in Gene Burnett's *Florida's Past* are narratives of the canal boondoggle . . . the political football . . . the barge-ship-boat canal. We're grateful to Gene for his in-depth work.

With a low bow to our English cousins, who for a couple centuries or so created gently Anglicized versions of our U.S. history, let's move to the chapter on history.

CHAPTER 3

The History

AN OVERVIEW—FROM DISCOVERY TO STATEHOOD

Welcome to a new kind of history, dedicated to folks who enjoy history but who don't want to work quite so hard at it.

It's history, all right, just not necessarily the kind we got in school.

It's a happy-go-lucky history full of people, plus a chronology of things for folks who like to take things real serious-like.

The 873,946 facts in these pages derive from hundreds of interviews, twenty-five years of speaking engagements, and over two hundred publications of every type, all about Florida's incredible history. Biased? You bet. Some of our 869,463 facts show Florida with about five hundred years in her history file . . . a hundred years or so more than the rest of the country.

Some facts have been lost to antiquity; some are reversed; some may seem wrong. Some may *be* wrong; some have been changed by our beloved English cousins.

At any rate, the fact that man roamed the Everglades some thirty thousand years ago gives us as good a place to start as any for a sojourn through Florida history.

A superfast chronology will show that the Spanish began Florida's modern history in 1513, with ol' Ponce stepping ashore that Easter Sunday and naming the whole place. (Remember, this is a thousand years per minute, so keep up.)

Anyway, Spain kept her for almost exactly 250 years. It was probably a lot of headaches, if the truth were known.

Spain's 250-year visit resulted in three tiny settlements, Pensacola, Fernandina, and St. Augustine, plus a string of little missions between the three. Then Spain swapped her to the English for Cuba, as part of the settlement of the French and Indian War (1763). Talk about a trade deal!

The British established two separate republics, East and West Florida, stretching from the Atlantic to the Mississippi River, and northward up through parts of the present-day states of Alabama and Mississippi. During the Revolutionary War, East Florida rejected an invitation to join the Colonies. Instead, it went its own way as an independent nation, raising its own flag and organizing its own militia, even repulsing an attack on its border by troops from Georgia.

England kept Florida for twenty years, headaches and all, then swapped her back to Spain, settling up for the Revolutionary War. They swapped her for the Bahamas, for heaven's sake.

Spain was looking for gold. Years later, the Binder Boys would have the same problem. Spain didn't seem to want her too badly, and in a couple years "welcomed" foreign settlers who might help clear some land. (Spain really was looking for gold, not swamp.) Tom Jefferson indicated that the new nation could have probably absorbed Florida, if they'd really wanted to . . . everybody was just so busy.

Anyway, Spain gave her back to the Colonies, via the British, following the War of 1812. This deal took almost two years to complete, probably because, for the first time, somebody had to come up with some cash! The new U.S. gave Spain $5 million to seal the deal. Florida finally became a U.S. territory in 1821 and a state in 1845. As the saying goes, "the rest is history."

IT'S POP-QUIZ TIME, BUT THIS DOES NOT COUNT TOWARDS YOUR GRADE

Let's check out a brief Florida true or false quiz, just to see if you're paying attention (and to see how much work we have to do).

By the way, all these items fall under the heading, "Things We Thought We Knew Till Now." So you know all the answers. We've been taught them for 300 years or so. Circle either *True* of *False* for each item (based on those 300 years), and watch for some exciting new slants on "Things We Thought, etc."

1) True or False—Columbus discovered America.

2) True or False—Columbus named America for Amerigo Vespucci, an Italian explorer whom he admired.

3) True or False—When Hernando de Soto discovered the Mississippi River, he began his search at its mouth, sailing up-river.

4) True or False—St. Augustine is the oldest settlement on the North American continent.

5) True or False—St. Augustine has served under five flags, more than any other settlement.

6) True or False—The first white child born in America was Virginia Dare.

7) True or False—The Pilgrims at Plymouth Rock were the first Europeans to reach the New World, fleeing religious persecution.

8) True or False—Capt. John Smith was saved from death at the hands of his Indian captors by the chief's daughter, Pocahontas, and later married her (the only decent thing to do).

9) True or False—Florida's first *real* real-estate promoter was the Marquis de Lafayette, following the Revolutionary War.

10) True or False—Gasparilla was the swashbuckling pirate who roamed the Gulf coast, king of all the pirates.

11) True or False—The first shot fired in the Civil War was at Ft. Sumter in the harbor at Charleston.

12) True or False—A young, foreign correspondent in the Spanish-American War later became prime minister of Great Britain.

13) True or False—The world's first commercial airline was developed by the Wright Brothers.

14) True or False—Henry Ford, when he raced his car at Daytona in 1904, stayed in the luxury suite at the Ormond Inn.

15) True or False—Presidential candidate William Jennings Bryan was once a real-estate promoter in Florida.

Now, let's take a look at some of the facts surrounding all these items we've all known and loved for lo, these many years. We hope you marked your answers in pencil.

HOW DID YOU DO?

1) As every schoolchild knows, Columbus discovered America, right? Well, not necessarily. Columbus discovered a ton of places—Cuba, Puerto Rico, Hispaniola, the Bahamas—but stepping ashore in our "America" was not to be his destiny.

2) Now about that naming business. Probably the most obscure man in all history, along with Whistler's father, has to be Martin Waldseemuller. Martin ran a little mapmaking shop in Germany. He was just a guy trying to get along.

Anyway, Martin was working away, copying some maps—reports say from 1497 to 1509—and he got this great idea. He had always admired the explorer Amerigo Vespucci, so he decided to stick his idol's name someplace on a new map he was lettering, instead of the name Columbus, which was supposed to go on the map. He also meant the name for what turned out to be South America. The printing was in dispute for years, thought to be a misspelled word.

So we feel it's high time old Waldseemuller got at least a little bit of credit.

The landmass turned out to be a continent, not an island, as everybody thought. There were no water passages to the Indies, China, or Japan.

3) As every schoolchild knows, the discovery of the Mississippi River was by Hernando de Soto. What we don't usually learn is that, in spring 1539, de Soto began his search for the Father of Waters from—of all places—Tampa Bay.

From the bay area, de Soto sent some of his troops marching overland, with the rest sailing along the coast. Both groups were to meet in the known area of Panza-Cola Bay and continue their search for the Mississippi. The route of the overland group, now termed the de Soto Trail, follows a wandering path all through Florida, including present-day Inverness, Ocala, Gainesville, Lake City, and into Tennessee,

Alabama, and back to the Tallahassee area. (Much of the de Soto Trail, incredibly enough, traces the outline of the cross-Florida canal discussed in the previous chapter.) The group finally arrived at the Mississippi on May 8, 1541.

There, the surviving troops built rafts from what material they had to navigate the river. Many died that winter, including Juan Ortiz, he of the "Pocahontas story" up ahead, as well as their leader. De Soto was secretly buried in the river to avoid upsetting the Indians, who thought he was a god.

Along their way, de Soto's men would have come upon a vast lake, called "the sink," Alachua Lake, just south of Gainesville. Later, in the 1880s, that giant lake would offer boating, picnics, and even a stop on the railroad. Today, it is Paine's Prairie.

Our appreciation to Melanie Barr, Gainesville historian, for her research and assistance regarding the history of the vast "lake that might come again," and for her material on the de Soto Trail.

4) Long before there was a Jamestown (1607), Florida was making history. In 1559, Pensacola had been settled by Tristan de Luna and 2,000 people. They made three attempts to establish their town, but were beset by Indians and hurricanes, in no particular order. They finally laid the site to rest for many years, thus losing forever the title, "oldest permanently occupied site in the New World."

The Spanish had settled Fernandina and the French Ft. Caroline (now Jacksonville), by 1560 and 1562. In 1565, the French colony was wiped out by the Spanish from their new fort at St. Augustine, confirming the Spanish hold on the New World.

So now Florida has not only the oldest site, but the four oldest sites: Pensacola, Fernandina, Ft. Caroline, and St. Augustine. And remember, just two years later, in 1567, Menendez sailed around the peninsula, leaving a fifth tiny mission on today's Miami Beach, and a sixth, near Ft. Myers, where he left those four Gaspar Brothers.

They'll come up later.

5) Fernandina has served under eight flags, all while a part of La Florida: France, Spain (twice), England (twice), Florida, Mexico, the American patriots, the Confederacy, and the United States (before and after the Civil War).

6) About that Virginia Dare matter; it's 1590, and Englisher John White and settlers step ashore in Virginia, seeking colonists they had left behind three years before to establish a settlement that would have predated Jamestown by twenty years. They find only remains of a campfire, some footprints, and no trace of the settlers, who passed into history as the Lost Colony.

White's daughter, Eleanor, who was married to his assistant, Ananiasta Dare, was one of two pregnant women among the group. It was their daughter Virginia who became the first English child born on the continent. The key word is *English,* since by that time, St. Augustine was well into its second generation of some three hundred families, with Pensacola and Fernandina adding to the population explosion. We just have to give credit where credit is due.

7) The history of America began with the Pilgrims, Plymouth Rock, Miles Standish, Priscilla and John, and the little ship *Mayflower,* right? Almost every Florida depression kid remembers being in the school play and playing either a Pilgrim, an Indian, Miles, John, or Priscilla (some of us were trees). Anyway, we all know that that's how it all started.

Well, not quite. Almost a hundred years before all these good folk came along, Ponce de Leon was stepping ashore, and naming La Florida—and Cape Canaveral. He thought it was a huge island. And while the Pilgrims were building tiny log huts to ward off the cold, St. Augustinians were starting to plan a major fort that would cost $30 million to build, and that would never be taken in battle.

One thing is sure, though. The Pilgrims were the first people to reach these shores while fleeing religious persecution. We know that.

Well, not really. About sixty years before the Pilgrims, French Huguenots settled a high bluff on the St. Johns River, overlooking a place that would someday be called Jacksonville. In 1562 they were fleeing severe religious persecution, but in a couple of seasons they'd be facing the Spanish in a fight for their turf.

8) As every schoolchild knows, Capt. John Smith, a captive of the Indians, was saved from death by Pocahontas, daughter of the chief, and later married her. As pictures portray, she flung her body over his to ward off the chopper's axe,

The curves of the St. Johns River created the perfect spot for the settlement of Ft. Caroline, which has now grown into the booming great city of Jacksonville. (Photo by Judy Jacobsen Photographic Service, Jacksonville)

and later became the bride of the intrepid explorer. It's a wonderful tale that has been taught to American children for hundreds of years.

Given enough research time, we find various works that contribute ingredients to the tale: A) In sum, Smith was not a prisoner at all, but a guest of Chief Powhatan. Some sources report that the chief later visited England. B) Ergo, Smith was never subject to the chopper's axe at all. C) And when Smith was in Virginia, Pocahontas (not her real name, by the way) was a charming, young lady—very young. She was four years old.

The story was created by a journalist friend of Smith's, Sir John Rolfe. *He* got it from a reporter, Richard Hakluyt, who had heard the tale from Portuguese seamen who did, indeed, tell the wondrous tale from the New World. Rolfe simply adapted the story to his friend. Smith denied the story repeatedly, telling his colleagues no such event ever occurred, especially involving someone with the unlikely name of Pocahontas.

However, the story Rolfe heard actually *did* occur. Guess where. In Florida! And about a hundred years earlier.

Another young officer, Capt. Juan Ortiz, travelling with deNarvaez on that Tampa Bay exploration in the 1520s, *was* seized by Indians, *was* sentenced to death, and *was* saved from death by the chief's daughter and wife! Now there's a story.

This Captain Juan apparently married the chief's daughter, and stayed with the tribe for nearly a decade, until he was accidentally discovered by de Soto, who was exploring along, at the time, looking for—of all things—the Mississippi River.

As one raffish historian said, "If we had the facts, we'd probably find Ortiz' wife was along with de Soto looking for her husband. . . ."

Ortiz' story caught on in the literary wateringholes of London. It found its way into print in the "news gazettes" of the day, and grew and grew. Finally, years later, Rolfe decided to visit Virginia to see for himself the setting of his creation, the John Smith Myth. Which he did.

Now, guess who really married Pocahontas.

You got it. Sir John Rolfe, that old scalawag, brought her back to England and presented his lady at court, where she enjoyed some attention, being an actual, authorized, card-carrying Indian princess!

And Florida's Captain Juan Ortiz entered the Grand Society of History's Unknowns. He attended regular meetings, presided over, of course, by Whistler's Father.

By the way, there's another Pocahontas story, also in Florida. This one took place in the Wakulla/Panhandle area. This time, the Pocahontas role was played by the daughter of Chief Proffitt Frances, and the "John" is a young Georgia militiaman at a local fort.

The soldier had gone hunting, had strayed onto tribal lands, was seized by Indians, was tried before the chief, and was sentenced to die for trespassing and poaching.

Although burning at the stake seems a bit stern for trespassing, folks looked at things a bit differently in those days.

Anyway, the chief's daughter begged for the soldier's life. It worked; the soldier was set free. He was later said to have married the princess, which certainly seems like the least he could do.

9) Florida's first *real* real-estate promoter, Le Général Marquis de Lafayette, was given a vast land grant in 1790 by a grateful U.S., for his help in the war. The tract was for anywhere he chose. He chose Florida, but he never saw the land. He sold it to friends, who resold it, etc.

10) "Gasparilla" is really Jose Gaspar. You'll find lots of juicy details on him before this chapter is over.

11) Pensacola says that first shot was at Ft. Pickens, not at Sumter at all, and that Sumter surrendered without a shot.

12) A young, foreign correspondent, staying at Henry Plant's new Tampa Bay Hotel, made his living selling stories to his hometown papers. His hometown was London . . . and the young correspondent's name was Winston Churchill.

13) The world's first commercial airline flight, passenger and all, took place in St. Petersburg, as the Tampa Bay Airlines began operations. Pilot Tony Jannus, flying his Benoist airboat, with St. Petersburg Mayor A. C. Pheil as the world's first airline passenger, flew from St. Pete to Tampa.

14) Henry Ford was too poor to stay in the Ormond Inn. He slept in his car.

15) It is true that William Jennings Bryan was involved in promoting real estate in Florida.

The world's first passenger airline flight took off from St. Petersburg and flew to Tampa on New Year's Day 1914. Crowds wished it well on takeoff, just as they cheered its arrival in Tampa across the bay. (Courtesy Florida State Photographic Archives)

Just keep this gentle thought. Some items in our history books, memorized by generations of children, may have been preceded by similar events on Florida soil.

With a giant thank you to the great researchers and historians, and to all our historical societies across Florida for their work and studies, let's take another look at some more items in our History Full of People and Things We Thought We Knew Till Now.

FLORIDA IN THE REAL OLDEN DAYS

Dr. John Gifford of the University of Miami's history experts has dredged up 12,000 years of history from Little Salt Springs, near the Myakka River in Sarasota County. He has found artifacts from another world, which were uncovered during the last Ice Age. Great glaciers formed and melted, raising and lowering the ocean's level, creating inland springs that simply burbled up from the ground in what had been a desertlike landscape. Little Salt Springs was one of these.

In the region, archaeologists have found remains of a tortoise, lying on its back, with charcoal bits under its shell and a spear-stake lodged between its upper and lower shell. Ancient hunters, Paleo-Indians, had apparently cooked the giant where it fell. Carbon-dating traced the find to 12,000 years ago.

Also found was a well-preserved "hunting boomerang," intricately shaped from a piece of oak, the first such weapon ever found on the continent. It dated back 9,000 years. The boomerang was used by Paleo-Indians to kill small game. Nearby was the base of a curved oak mortar, used in grinding meal.

The study of Florida's ancient history is virtually just getting underway, largely through efforts of dedicated researchers such as Dr. Gifford and his colleagues.

The University of Miami team has noted that natural springs, such as Little Salt, became major Ice-Age gathering spots for both man and animal. The giant mammoth, giant sloth, saber-toothed tiger, and other creatures sought water sources, and nomadic hunters followed.

Over fifty natural springs dot the central Florida landscape (there are over two hundred springs in the entire state—

more than at any other single location on Earth). The warm, mineral waters provided the perfect preservative for wood and other organic matter. Normally, wood rots over the centuries. However, at Little Salt Springs, the water is so old and comes from such a deep source in solid rock that there is almost no oxygen content; thus bacteria cannot survive in order to decompose organic matter. In short, anything that has ever fallen or was thrown into Little Salt Springs remains extremely well preserved.

Little Salt and other similar locations contain the most important underwater discoveries in the history of man. Recent efforts have developed to explore sites far below the now well known "tortoise-ledge" findings. The deeper the explorers go in the incredibly preserving mineral waters, the older the times discovered. Some 250 feet down, where divers may only work a few minutes at a time, Gifford theorizes it may be possible eventually to reach the epoch when man first began to roam this hemisphere—estimated to be twenty to thirty thousand years ago.

In one instance, the Gifford team found submerged human bodies, covered by a dense peat base which had kept oxygen out entirely. The 12,000-year-old Paleo-Indian tortoise killers remained virtually intact. In this 1986 find of buried Indians, the skull of a young woman was unearthed. The skull's brain tissue, which had been literally frozen by the waters, was still undecomposed. The explorers had to refreeze the tissue instantly with liquid nitrogen; as Dr. Gifford found, once such tissue is exposed to the air, it begins to crumble in one's hands. This skull was estimated to be 7,000 years old.

We can only guess what the coming hundred years or even fifty years of exploration will turn up. Just as explorers of a half-thousand years ago searched Florida's magic lands for hidden treasures, in the coming century, we may be sure treasures will continue to be found.

LET'S TALK ABOUT THAT PENSACOLA AND ST. AUGUSTINE BUSINESS

St. Augustine, the oldest continuously occupied site on the continent, with its charm and stability, is always accorded the "oldest city" name. It has the oldest schoolhouse, oldest house, oldest streets, probably the oldest street signs, and maybe even the oldest fire hydrants, although, if memory serves, Cleveland has the oldest streetlights. Oh well.

It simply has all the history one can absorb.

Ft. Caroline was older than that, but in 1562, within months following the French settlement there, Spanish troops under Menendez were ordered to establish a fort and remove the French interlopers, since Spain had claimed all the territory as far as the eye could see, and as far back as 1513. The Spanish did exactly as ordered, actually massacring the entire French force. The slaughter took place at the Matanzas River, so named by the Spanish as "Place of Slaughter."

But in West Florida, Pensacolians will quickly—and repeatedly—remind you that their city is really the original settlement on the continent, with Tristan de Luna arriving with 2,000 settlers on August 14, 1559, from Vera Cruz, only to be met by a roaring, savage hurricane followed by hostile Indians.

Now, 450 years later, the "Mother-in-Law of the Navy" (so many young men find brides during their naval aviator training) boasts the world's first naval air station, begun in 1914.

Lindbergh stopped here to repair his barn-storming plane. Even "The Lady Who Would Be Queen" began her colorful career here, when she dated and married her first of three husbands, a young Lt. Winfield Spencer. She was Miss Wallis Warfield of Baltimore.

Your Pensacola tour must include the Naval Air Station; Trader Jon's; the great historic Seville Square; Ft. Pickens, where Geronimo was imprisoned; the glorious bays and beaches; and the fantastic Naval Air Museum, destined to become one of the finest air museums in the world.

Pensacola reenacts de Luna's landing in 1559 each year. St. Augustine produces its Passion play, *The Cross and Sword,* each year, reenacting Menendez' settling in 1565 . . . with Fernandina and Ft. Caroline somewhere in between.

Pensacola bombards visitors with brochures, guidebooks, and history folders. St. Augustine counters with brochures, guidebooks, and history folders.

At Florida's "first city," Pensacola, a "must-see" is the world's first Naval Air Museum, and probably the largest, with some two hundred aircraft on display. This is just one of the display areas. (Courtesy Naval Aviation Museum Foundation)

It's been amiably said in Pensacola that most bad things in town are "probably the work of St. Augustine spies." It's been said in St. Augustine that "old de Luna didn't stick in there like we did." But approximately every third Pensacolian one meets will be quick to remind visitors that "St. Augustine is our charming, younger sister."

We are indebted to native Pensacolian/historian Virginia Parks, editor of "Pensacola Historical Society Publication" and author of the delightful book *Pensacola: Spaniards to Space Age,* for providing such great insights into West Florida's premier harbor town.

Let us move forward to discover some more remarkable facts about the history of our own La Floreeda. Come on along. You might enjoy the trip.

AT LAST—A FLORIDA CHRONOLOGY

Patrick Carr, in his probing book, *Sunshine States,* provides the consummate study of Florida's future problems, in water, waste, and population, with emphasis on the Tampa Bay region. We mention this not only because of the writer's skills, but because of a reviewer's comment in a national publication. Carr, himself, may learn of the comment for the first time, in these pages. The reviewer, apparently scanning the book and unaware of the fact that Carr had digested more of the Tampa Bay "feel" in a couple seasons than many old Crackers have in many generations, summed up the book with: "It's a shame Carr did not provide us with a chronology of Florida. One is needed. . . ." or words to that effect.

Patrick, in appreciation for your work on the Bay, if any reviewer ever asks you for a chronology, give 'em this one. It should be enough for almost anyone. There ought to be a Writer's Law: one chronology per lifetime.

While no record can be perfect, we've included items from virtually every segment of Florida's history: population, culture, business, growth, civics, society, and persons drawn from all parts of the magic land.

1490—Columbus plans and seeks financing for voyages.

1492—Columbus's first voyage makes landfall at present-day Watling Island, Bahamas, his nearest point to "America."

1493—Columbus's second voyage; young officer, Ponce de Leon, is left behind as governor of "The Puerto Rico Islands."

1497—The Cabots, John and Sebastian, possibly visit Florida. Create several maps said to have been used by Ponce on later trips.

1500—Three more voyages by Columbus and associates. They settle coastlines from Honduras to Mexico—seventeen towns on Hispaniola alone—plus Jamaica and Cuba. Columbus opened the New World. Ponce de Leon, still governor of Puerto Rico, loses job to Diego, Columbus's brother.

1513—Ponce, now an out-of-work explorer, is told by the king, "Ponce, you can be governor of the Beminis." Ponce tours Florida coast, searching for the Beminis. Finds Cape Canaveral, names the entire place La Florida, and claims it for Spain. Spain will keep her for 250 years.

1521—Ponce's last tour brings priests to convert Indians. They tour the Keys and Gulf Coast, possibly all the way to Texas and Mexico. Entire continent is still considered La Florida (they probably still thinks it's a giant island). Florida at this time runs from the Rio Grande to the Carolinas. Ponce's ship is wrecked in Charlotte Harbor. Ponce is wounded by Indians and dies.

1528—Panfilo deNarvaez, the next explorer, visits Tampa Bay. Young Capt. Juan Ortiz is captured by Indians, saved from death by daughter and wife of chief, marries daughter, lives with tribe 9 years; this is the real Pocahontas story you've been hearing about for the past 375 years.

1520s—Verrazano, for whom a big bridge would be named years later in some place called New York, explores entire Atlantic coast of Florida. New York hadn't been invented yet.

1539—Hernando de Soto leaves Pizarro in Peru, sails into Tampa Bay, and sends troops inland to hunt for Mississippi River. Troops find Juan Ortiz instead. Take him along. No record as to whether Juan wanted to go or not.

De Soto priests observe first Christmas Mass in New World, Tampa Bay area. De Soto settles South Tampa Bay. Today's giant De Soto Oak, which casts a shadow of 100 feet, is said to have been standing when de Soto arrived there.

1558-59—Tristan de Luna sails from Vera Cruz with ships,

soldiers, and 2,000 settlers. Lands at Pensacola Bay. Tries to settle three times. Gives it up as a bad neighborhood.

1560—Establishment of Fernandina, second oldest settlement on continent.

1562-64—Settlement of Ft. Caroline by French, near mouth of St. Johns River.

1565—Menendez de Aviles ordered by King Philip to settle St. Augustine and "take care" of the French nearby. He does, thus giving Florida the first, second, third, and fourth oldest settlements.

1600—Tiny Spanish missions settled, trying to connect St. Augustine and Pensacola to bind empire together.

1660s—St. Augustine lays plans for building of Castillo de San Marcos, which will become oldest fortification on continent.

1696—St. Augustine completes fort: cost $30 million and boasts walls thirty feet thick. The fort is often tested, but never taken. Is later named Ft. Marion, for Revolutionary War hero Gen. Francis Marion, the Old Swamp Fox. Also in 1696, Jonathan Dickinson is shipwrecked off the southeast coast with a party of Quakers; is escorted by Indians up entire Eastern U.S. wilderness to Philadelphia, unharmed. He gives us Florida's oldest English place name.

1700s—Queen Anne's War—Governor Moore of Georgia invades and burns St. Augustine. Tries to take the fort but cannot. King George's War—Oglethorpe invades St. Augustine. Tries to take fort but fails.

1715—Beginning of Great Plate Fleet—fleet laden with gold and treasure, guarded by Spanish warships, sailing up Florida "Gold Coast" bound for Spain. It averages $10 million in transported treasure each year for nearly a century.

1715-85—Estimated fifteen thousand ships lie on the bottom of Gold Coast, sunk by hurricanes and pirates, awaiting treasure-hunters two centuries ahead.

THE LEGEND OF THE GASPARS

Speaking of pirates, let's take a break from our chronology to get a closer look at one mind-bending pirate legend. Jose Gaspar gives Florida one of its most incredible tales.

Gasparilla! Swashbuckling aristocrat, mutineer, pirate! Well, let's just see!

Let's take it from the top:

1756—Tiny Jose Gaspar is born in Barcelona. All records begin to disappear.

1776 (estimated)—Young Gaspar becomes naval cadet in Royal Spanish Navy; more records immediately disappear. He becomes a restless, high-spirited young officer, ready for action.

1777 (estimated)—(A lot of dates become estimated at this point.) Conspires with fellow cadets to steal a Spanish warship. Now there's a cadet prank for you.

1778 (estimated)—Gang decides to move to Florida for the winter, settles on Gulf Coast, and sets up career in pirating, feeling it has a high return on investment. Gaspar names himself as president and CEO of the firm, develops Employee Relations Committee, and joins the Chamber.

1779—Sets up headquarters in Ft. Myers/Port Charlotte/ Sanibel/Captiva/Boca Grande/Gasparilla Island—take your choice. Also names all these places (Sanibel was his sweetheart, the sister of one of his officers, and he later planned to marry her, or seduce her . . . take your choice! Names Captiva Island for his captive wives, whom he seized in pirate raids, and whom he doesn't need to seduce). Builds pirate empire. Business is very good, especially in season.

1783—Named "king of the pirates," a sort of Benny Goodman of the Gulf Coast set. Amasses huge pirate fortune, estimated at thirty million dollars—a lot of money in those days, even on Sanibel and Captiva. Keeps it buried all over the place. Didn't trust banks.

1800 (estimated)—Names Useppa Island for his favorite wife, Joseffe, niece of Napoleon. Keeps her separate from other wives.

1821 (probably about 3 P.M. or 1500 hours, if you prefer)— Lookouts spy innocent British merchant ship; decide to have one last fling before retiring. Gaspar loads up the gang, all except the digging crew, which stays behind, digging. He probably says, "Keep the beer cold. We'll be right back," or whatever pirates say on such occasions. Sails out to ravage passing ship. Now the plot begins to thicken, so try to keep calm. Probably about 4 P.M. or 1600 hours, the merchant ship, spying Gaspar, unwraps a ton of guns and hoists flag revealing itself to be . . . are you ready . . . the U.S. gunboat *Enterprise*! (Probably going where no man has gone before.) About 5 P.M. the *Enterprise* shoots Gaspar's ship to shreds. Gaspar, sensing trouble, wraps himself in anchor chain and hurls self overboard, where he promptly drowns. About 6:30 P.M. the *Enterprise* kills all of Gaspar's crew, except for ten guys whom they take back to New Orleans to be hanged. Some choice. The only survivors are those six guys back on the island, digging up that $30 million in treasure. Now there's some good duty for you! Nothing is ever heard from those six guys again. Nothing is ever heard from the $30 million, either. (You think they were going to turn it in at Tallahassee? Tallahassee hadn't been invented yet.)

This is truly one of the fantastic stories of Florida's fantastic history . . . but wait! There's even more.

Gaspar had the finest of good old pirate names: Gasparilla! Some reports discuss his physical appearance, saying he was tall. Since Gasparilla means "Little Gaspar," we seem to have a tall yet little swashbuckling Gaspar. You pays your money and you takes your choice.

In 1904, Tampa's social leaders adopted the pirate as their "mascot" for a celebration. The event caught on so well that it became an annual tradition, growing into the Ye Mystic Krewe of Gasparilla, which now includes over seven hundred city leaders. It grew into Tampa's three-day gala, the Gasparilla Festival, with the tall, Gasparilla ship sailing into the bay, seizing the city, then liberating it, accompanied by much general merrymaking all saluting the dashing Gaspar.

Now we're going to take you on a tour of just where all the Gaspar stories come from. Stick around. It may prove interesting, certainly as interesting as Columbus. And Gaspar didn't say he discovered anyplace; he just named them all.

If you're new in the neighborhood, we hate to be the ones to break the news, but most Florida historians will know that all of the foregoing incredible story is just that: a story. The fact about stories is that, over the years, stories begin to become fact. The legend of Gasparilla that we have just outlined is considered fact by "Armed Camp #1," and fiction by

At Tampa's famed Gasparilla Festival, "Gaspar's" ship and crew sail into Tampa Bay, seize the city, liberate it, and put on a whale of a party. (Courtesy Tampa/Hillsborough Convention and Visitors Association)

"Armed Camps #2-3-4-5." Each of these has its own version of the Gaspar story.

Armed Camp #2 says that all of the above took place from Gaspar's birth in 1756 to that big beach party we told you about, and that Gaspar really did name all those great places—Sanibel, Captiva, and the rest—all around 1821, in fact.

However, Armed Camp #2 points out that all those place names, the islands, passes, sound, all were on maps about two hundred years before Gaspar was born!

The names were said to have been on maps, clear back to 1567. That's when Menendez, after settling St. Augustine, sailed around Florida and established a tiny mission in the Ft. Myers area, leaving four diminutive priests to take care of the place. Remember that all four of the priests were named Gaspar!

The priests began to place names on maps and sketches, making reference to themselves: St. Ybel (Sanibel), Gasparilla Key (Island and Sound also), even Captiva and Useppa. Menendez himself was said to have named a couple places.

Along comes Armed Camp #3, which says, "Sure, now we have five Gaspars altogether, and they were probably related!" Now, there's a new direction. Even Armed Camp #1 never came up with this idea.

Maybe they were related. But that would have made the priests the ancestors of the pirate. Naaahhh, not even in Florida.

Now Armed Camp #4 tells of that final pirate junket, back at the beach party with that ship the *Enterprise*. Well, U.S. Navy records show that the *Enterprise*, on that date, logged off the coast of Jamaica, 1,000 miles away from the party. So much for that item.

Finally, Armed Camp #5 has the simplest, least exciting story of the legendary, swashbuckling pirate, and that is that he never buckled a single swash!

The entire story of Gaspar the pirate apparently was invented by a railroad press agent named Johnny Gomez. Gomez dreamed up the story to go on the front cover of his new ticket-brochure for the old Charlotte and Northern Railroad, where he worked. He had seen the name in books, heard it in stories, seen it on the land, and simply made up the pirate tales out of thin air—pure, thin Cracker air.

Rail officials liked the idea so much, they used it for the brochure, expanded the story, and made it their official "logo" for the company. They even began to include Gomez in the fable as it grew. The story was so successful, Gomez' role in the legend was promoted. Company officials began to include Johnny in the stories as a cabin boy; then as an ordinary seaman; then as Gaspar's personal guide; then as executive officer; and finally as "assistant admiral," whatever that may be. Eventually, Gomez was even named as Gaspar's brother-in-law!

So, for this Armed Camp, it all began with a simple railroad ticket-brochure.

The incredible part of the story is that Johnny Gomez actually did exist, and did do all the above.

Gomez was—at many times—many things: railroad press agent; soldier of fortune; fishing guide in the Keys, where he lived on Panther Key. He was said to be America's oldest living man, age 119, 120, 121, 122—you takes your choice. Anyway, at 119, 120, 121, 122, Gomez, fishing for mullet in his small boat, became entangled in *his* anchor rope, was pulled overboard, and was drowned.

From that final beer bust on the beach, to the great "anchor-chain/anchor-rope" twin drownings (good dramatic touch), Hemingway couldn't have done it better. It is all fiction.

Or is it?

With so many accounts of Gaspar from so many sources, it is difficult to dismiss the entire fable out of hand. When such a work as the prestigious "Official Bicentennial Commemorative Book of Florida," with its major-name authors, deigns to acknowledge the Gaspar stories, even if only to refute most of them, it is worth looking into.

Prime among the many sources must be the Gasparilla Festival itself, for nearly a century one of Tampa's most spectacular events. Here, the festival committee and its brochure have Jose serving as a lieutenant in the Spanish Navy for five years apparently, then swiping that warship. (Tampa's sources *do* point out that few real facts are known of the famed swashbuckler.)

Other accounts, allegedly quoting Jose's own diary, report his capture of thirty-six—count 'em—thirty-six ships during his first twelve years as a pirate. You gotta make your numbers or clean out your desk in this game, mister.

Crews of captured ships were given the option of joining Gaspar's ranks, or walking the plank. Fates of captured ladies apparently were determined by the pirate's whim of the moment.

Tampa's stories do include the attack on the *Enterprise* and the famed anchor-chain drowning. However, not content with having Jose simply jump overboard wrapped in his anchor chain (which probably contributed to his drowning), the festival report has the pirate "brandishing his sword in a final gesture of defiance . . . as he sinks beneath the surface." Way to go, Jose!

The festival report also indicates that Gaspar was well suited to his calling. He was a Spanish nobleman, adventurous, fierce, a born leader, well educated, with courtly manners . . . a fine gentleman and yet a bit of a rogue. Wow!

Tampa even adds in a "Lopez," as a beloved first mate to Gaspar, his dedicated executive officer. "Lopez" even *retires,* and is allowed to borrow a ship to sail back home to Spain. Hey, the ol' boss-pirate not only had class, but was a pushover for a persuasive executive officer!

Could this "Lopez" also be Johnny Gomez, in a typographical error, like Amerigo was? (These typos can really mess things up!)

In another incident, Gaspar is reported to have captured a ship and found that its commander was a certain Captain Menendez, a classmate of his back at the old academy. Oh *come on, now!* Anyway, Gaspar is so pleased to see old Manny after all these years (Gaspar never went to class reunions), he takes him back to HQ—probably at Boca Grande, Sanibel, or Captiva (probably Captiva, where the ladies were)—and extends him every courtesy.

But wait. There's more. And here's where it really chokes you up.

Eventually, Menendez dies . . . from hurling his body between Gaspar and an attacker, a disgruntled crew member about to stab the sleeping pirate. There's a slow fade into the sunset for you! It's almost as good as those six guys back on the island counting that $30 million treasure.

Now, as if all this were not enough, comes incredible research and "digging" (literally) by writers L. Frank Hudson and Gordon R. Prescott from Joyce Allyn's Great Outdoors Publishing Co., of St. Petersburg. Hudson and Prescott include in their works detailed reports of: A) Gaspar's palatial mansions on what is now Boca Grande, filled with paintings and tapestries. B) His communications network with his crews on another island. C) His entertainments in the grand fashion. D) His ordering construction of 100 oaken chests, lined with copper, to hold his treasure. The authors report having seen the bill of sale for these items. E) His settlements on the other islands; his troops' quarters; and his "competitors," the Bocilla Brothers, who reigned a few hundred yards across the inlet in what is now the hamlet of Bokeelia at the very north tip of Pine Island. F) Gaspar's diary, currently hidden away in a Castro-Cuban library.

So, whether based on fact or fiction, the famed Gasparilla Festival in Tampa will remain in the memories of thousands as one of Florida's truly great parties! Perhaps someday, someone will hold a "Johnny Gomez Festival."

There still is another source to be heard from: our esteemed colleague, British satirist-humorist-cartoonist Richard Harris, in his London studios where he is researching a book of cartoon satire on Gaspar and other "famous pirates of the world," a sort of *Pirates' Who's Who*.

Richard has been good enough to share items with us for these pages. His research parallels our own and several others, pointing out: A) The U.S Navy records show the *Enterprise*—on December 21, 1821—being nowhere near Sanibel or Captiva but near Jamaica, 1,000 miles away. B) The Spanish Royal Navy shows no record of a Jose Gaspar ever having been a cadet, and no record of any warship ever having been stolen by anyone—at any time. C) Barcelona City Hall shows no record of a Jose Gaspar ever being born!

We salute all the great researchers for such noble efforts on Gaspar the pirate and the four Gaspar Brothers.

If we ever *do* find out what happened to those six guys they left behind digging up that $30 million, then we'll really have a story!

And so, as we fade into the sunset over Captiva (or Sanibel), and we see the tall pirate ship sailing to the horizon, perhaps there are six families living on Sanibel (or Captiva, or . . . oh, never mind) who *do* know the real story of Tall, Short, Little, Big Gaspar and his reign as king of all Florida's pirates. They probably know all about Johnny Gomez . . . even Roderigo Lopez, and even Menendez. But most importantly, they also know the real data on those six guys left behind on the island, as members of that "digging-up crew," securing that $30 mill.

If you're ever in the neighborhood and want to inquire, stop in and visit. Ask 'em about their great-grandparents. You can spot 'em easily. They'll be the ones living in those $6 million houses, and they smile a lot.

BACK TO OUR CHRONOLOGY

Now that we've finished examining the Gasparilla legend up close, it's time to return to our serious overall chronology of Florida history.

1763 — End of French and Indian War; Spain gives up Florida to England, ending her first 250 years reign of region. Those years resulted in fourteen tiny missions, four or five settlements, and a road to connect them all. Now British names begin to filter in: Amelia Island (Amelia was daughter of King George III), Fort George, Charlotte Harbor, Lake George.

1763-83 — England holds Florida and establishes two separate republics — East Florida and West Florida — ranging from the Atlantic seaboard to the Mississippi River and into parts of adjoining states.

1781 — Key West is owned by a single artillery officer. He sells it. Finally a Florida governor gives the island to another officer, who sells it to John Simonton for $2,000.

1783 — England, at close of Revolutionary War, loses Florida as part of its losses to Colonies. England swaps Florida interests for the Bahamas. Spain takes up where she left off, twenty years before. Spain begins new "thorn-in-side" relations with other Southern colonies through border disputes, slavery, raids, and harassment. Spain invites "foreigners" to move to Florida and settle the land. Jefferson indicates that Colonies could probably take Florida any time they wished, but nobody seems to want her at this point.

1790—Le Général Marquis de Lafayette, Florida's first *real* real-estate promoter, is given vast land grant by the U.S., and he takes a tract in Florida, sight unseen. Eventually sells to friends.

Florida begins "The Old Florida Doubling Game," doubling its population every couple of decades. Experts say it will stop by 1890. Then they said it would stop in 1980. Then in 1990.

1820-1842—Skirmishes, raids, and battles become the Seminole Indian Wars. The Seminole Nation maintains hostile relations with the U.S. until the final treaty settlement in 1976 (134 years, the longest such "war" in modern history).

1821—Spain begins to cede region back to England as settlement for the War of 1812. It takes two years to work the deal. Spain gets $5 million for all of Florida, plus other side deals. This ends 300 years of Florida's being a puppet, a pawn, probably even a pirate and a poet, too . . . a political football of nations striving for control of the Gulf region.

1821-22—Odet Phillippe pioneers Tampa Bay/Safety Harbour. Brings the grapefruit to Florida and the world from the Bahamas. Andrew Jackson named first military governor of Florida; sets his government up in Pensacola for West Florida, with Governor Duval to work in St. Augustine for East Florida. Decides they must find a common capital somewhere in between.

1822—American flag flies over Florida as it becomes a U.S. territory. Things start to pick up.

1824—President Monroe and two governors appoint two couriers—one from Pensacola and one from St. Augustine—to ride towards one another. Wherever they meet will be site of new capital. Becomes Talla-Hassee, meaning Old Town. For all you adopted Crackers and beloved snowbirds, now you know how the capital got to be way up there.

1824-30—Towns spring up along "St. Augustine Road" traversing North Florida: Chiefland, Perry, Sneads, Two Egg, Marianna, Chipley, Bonifay. This is the first land boom.

1800s—Young Lt. Zachary Taylor, during Florida duty, meets, courts, and marries charming lady named Davis. Zach becomes president of the United States, and later, his father-in-law, Jefferson Davis, is president of the Confederate States of America.

1833—Amalgam of many tribes enter Florida, fleeing dreaded "Trail of Tears" forced march of all Indians to Oklahoma. These "remnants" of workers, slaves, freedmen, and Indians become known by the Creek/Cherokee word "Seminole," meaning Wild Ones. Young chief Osceola becomes major Indian leader.

1837—Osceola comes to U.S. military under flag of truce. Is imprisoned at Ft. Moultrie, Georgia. Is beheaded; body displayed as his leadership comes to tragic end. This is a major black mark in the U.S. treatment of its first citizens. Wars cost U.S. $40 million and 1,400 lives before Seminoles finally settle into unreachable vastness of Everglades.

1838—First State Constitution signed at tiny town of St. Joseph. Most citizens had previously lived in nearby town of St. Marks, until it came under control of new landowners who raised all the rents. Folks just moved to St. Joseph. St. Joseph becomes Florida's largest city.

1841—St. Joseph decimated by a yellow fever epidemic and a hurricane. Survivors flee back to St. Marks. St. Joseph lies fallow for half-century until St. Joe Paper Company renames town as Port St. Joe, resurrecting fine city. In 1841, Apalachicola replaced dying St. Joseph as largest town on Gulf Coast, shifting Florida's population center.

1845—Florida becomes a state. Pioneer families settle in Alligator (Lake City), Corinth, Marianna, Chipley, Bonifay, and some smaller towns, too.

1850-60s—Jacksonville booms to 18,000 people, Florida's largest city. With new luxury hotels, it becomes a tourist mecca. Miami, however, is still a tiny cluster of three homes and outbuildings. Travellers, eventually to be called "tourists," have only found the northern edge of Florida so far.

1861—Florida is third state to leave the Union; joins Confederacy. Pensacola historians say the Civil War's "first shot" was not fired at Sumter, but at Ft. Pickens, Pensacola.

1864—Florida's Civil War battles—Olustee and Battle of Natural Bridge, in Marianna. Small boys and old wounded men fought the Federals in a battle with no military significance whatsoever. Bodies of children and even Union sympathizers were found after the fight.

1865—Florida forced to surrender. Begins reconstruction. Governor John Milton takes own life; prefers death to Reconstruction. Florida nearing bankruptcy, finances in chaos.

1868—Florida writes a new constitution, which stays in force for 100 years, until the 1968 Convention. Following Civil War, Florida faces default on state bonds; credit is risky.

1869—Jonathan C. Gibbs is first black secretary of state. His name survives in Gibbs High School, St. Petersburg.

1870—Green Cove Springs, the town with four "angels," grows into an attractive tourist hamlet with J. C. Penney, Mr. Hoover of vacuum cleaner fame, dairyman Gail Borden, and later President Grover Cleveland leading.

1875—Ormond Beach founded, planned as health resort for employees of a New Britain, Conn., lock company. Town and Ormond Inn become favorite of Flagler and his original oil partner, John D. Rockefeller.

1881—Hamilton Disston, the visionary "who saw too far into the future and who died too soon," comes to Florida with a promise of $1,000,000 cash for 4 million acres of swampland. His promise to pay helps bail out ailing state treasury. Plans to drain 6,000 square miles of Florida lands. He owns big chunk of South Florida. Sarasota founded; means "Place of Dancing." It's a beautiful town; a part of Disston's 4-million-acre land buy. First rails connect Sarasota and Tampa. Workers don't get paid. Come back in 1884 and rip up the rails (old-fashioned Cracker labor negotiations).

1883—Lake City becomes home of State Agriculture College, which remains there until 1905, when it is politically removed to Gainesville and becomes University of Florida. Original "Opera House," first in Florida, opens in Pensacola. Becomes a classic structure. Attracts major period entertainment to West Florida. Also in 1883, Flagler visits St. Augustine and eventually builds three hotels in town. His dynasty along the Atlantic seaboard is being established. Florida will never be the same.

1885—Henry Plant brings rails down Gulf Coast to Tampa (bypasses tiny Cedar Key). Florida is on its way and running. Also that year, St. Augustine becomes main tourist center, replacing Jacksonville, and becomes state's leading town.

1885-90—Flagler moves rails and hotels down Eastern seaboard. Moves down to Ormond Beach. Acquires huge Ormond Inn. Flagler founds Palm Beach, West Palm Beach, more rails, and more hotels.

1890—Key West becomes largest city in Florida, richest per capita in income level. Tourists find it's as far south as she goes.

1891—Plant builds monumental Tampa Bay Hotel, 1,200 feet long with a mile walk around the building. It becomes showplace of Tampa. Is present home of University of Tampa.

1892—Plant builds second monumental hotel: Belleview Biltmore. Helps build town of Belleair to hold hotel.

1893—Words "freeze" and "Great Freeze" come into Florida's language, helping bring (along with Mrs. Tuttle's orange blossom and nice note) Flagler to Miami.

1896—Miami begins to grow as Flagler brings rails and hotel to the tiny village at the behest of Julia Tuttle. The two "Titans," Flagler and Plant, race each other down opposite coasts of their 58,000-square-mile personal gameboard.

1897—Seaboard Airline Railway comes to Sarasota with S. Davies Warfield in charge. He is the "Uncle Sol" of Miss Wallis Warfield. Then the Spanish-American War comes to Tampa. Tampa Bay Hotel is headquarters; it has poured-concrete walls four feet thick, built to last for 100 years. It certainly has. Teddy Roosevelt says, " . . . wasn't much of a war, but it was the only one we had." Now 70,000 troops, "followers," promoters, and hustlers pour into Tampa (pop. 12,000). Merchants go wild; cannot stock shelves. Government contracts pour in. Personages include Teddy Roosevelt, his Rough Riders, William Jennings Bryan, artist Frederic Remington, and young war correspondent Winston Churchill. A third of Tampa's residents are Cuban cigar workers. Tampa becomes the foundation of Cuban independence, leading into the war.

1898—First telegraphed message of sinking of battleship *Maine* comes to tiny Punta Rassa, near Ft. Myers, thence to nation. Florida population doubles from two decades earlier.

1899—Flagler announces intention to make Florida his legal residence. His agents are alleged to have arranged for the

Florida legislature to pass what is called the "Flagler Divorce Law."

1901—Governor Jennings signs the bill. Flagler has wife placed in sanitarium in New York and divorces her under the new law. Marries Mary Lily Kenan, third Mrs. Flagler. Then the legislature rescinds the law. Only one divorce was ever granted under it. Roughly twenty to fifty thousand 1901 dollars probably changed hands to get this law passed in the first place, but the money and records disappeared.

Also in 1901, Lake City is given the handsome Flagler Gym by Flagler to serve University of Florida.

On May 3, 1901, the least known of all Florida calamities occurs: Great Fire of Jacksonville, caused by cigarette in mattress factory. Levels 130 square blocks of city. Soldiers patrol rubble. City rebuilds into new, grander showplace.

1900s—Population center of state has drifted from Jacksonville to St. Augustine, along with the rails, then to Key West, St. Petersburg, Tampa, St. Joseph, with all stops in between. The enigma of Florida begins. The Northern area becomes deeply "Southern" in philosophy and language. The Southern area becomes almost totally "Northern."

Jacksonville grows to become "The City of Governors," with eleven of Florida's governors coming from this one city: Kirk, Burns, Bryant, Jennings, Warren, Martin, Fleming, Drew, Reed, Broward, and DuVal, for whom the county is named.

1904—Henry Ford races his flivver at Daytona. Too poor to stay in Ormond Inn. Sleeps in car.

1904-12—Flagler creates "Railroad That Went to Sea" with 4,000 workers through five hurricanes. It costs hundreds of lives, but reaches Key West in 1912. The city holds a three-day celebration. Many had never seen a train.

1905—State moves University of Florida from Lake City to Gainesville.

1911—John Ringling adopts Sarasota area. The Ringling mansion, circus quarters, art collection, and museum are all given to the town at Ringling's death.

1913—Henry Flagler dies at ninety-three—his Overseas Railroad complete. End of an era, an epoch, for Florida's east coast giant.

1920s—Aircraft builder Glenn Curtiss arrives among hundreds of "boomers." Helps build two towns west of Miami: Opa-Locka, around the Arabian Nights theme, and Hialeah, around a horse-track. Florida's land boom creates economic fury; lasts ten years. Dwarfs all gold rushes put together (see "The Land Boom" chapter).

1926—First of two back-to-back "killer storms" begins to dampen fires of Florida's land boom.

1928—Tamiami Trail opens. For first time motorists are able to "loop" entire state. Creates first man-made barrier to natural flow of water over wetlands. This move will haunt naturalists decades later. Also, the '28 hurricane hits Okeechobee and scoops 770 square miles of water from the giant saucer. Wipes out town of Moore Haven. Ranks with Johnstown flood and Galveston storm as three worst U.S. disasters; about three thousand lives lost.

1930s—Famed CCC Boys—Civilian Conservation Corps—come to Florida. These young men plant over thirteen million trees in 200,000 acres of Florida. They cut miles of firebreaks. Are paid flat monthly amount plus "food and found."

The Florida population is stabilizing, with a dip in the growth rate caused by the great land boom and bust, the hurricanes of '26 and '28, the national stock market crash, and the great depression. These effects last until World War II, when thousands of servicemen on military assignment discover Florida and return after the war.

Florida is cross-stitched with old "macadam" roads, "nine feet wide and nine feet deep," referring to deep sand along the shoulders of tiny highways. Autos that meet swerve off the pavement to pass; the outside wheels go in the sand, often to stay. This prompts the classic Crackerism, "I think one of his tars is still in the sand" (in case anyone ever asks). We don't know where "most of his jelly done fell off his cracker" comes from.

1934-36—Countless Florida depression kids learn familiar numbers. For instance, twelve dollars per week uses the old arithmetic of thirty cents an hour times forty hours. Folks worked hard for this money. This brought protests from citrus and turpentine business owners, although they were paying less to laborers in a kind of fiefdom relationship.

Employers demanded a ruling that anyone refusing their nine dollars a week be barred from working relief "weed gangs" for twelve dollars. Folks were simply not "allowed" to go on relief.

We will limit our time travel to the period 1490 to 1940. The period past 1940 must wait its turn.

FLORIDA GOES TO WAR

While our time travel has rambled from 1490 to 1940, we must save a special place for World War II. With most headline action being in faraway places, Florida still became a vast armed camp during the period of 1940 to 1945. From Eglin Field in the Panhandle (the largest U.S. Air Force base in the world); to Pensacola, the world's first naval air station; to the huge army training base, Camp Blanding, near Starke; to Tampa's Drew Field and MacDill Field; to Cocoanut Grove's naval training base; to Jacksonville's Mayport; to Key West's navy subs; to Homestead Air Force Base; to the amphibious landing base at Ft. Pierce . . . the military spanned the state.

In addition, across the state, hundreds of hotels were commandeered for the military, for active duty, for training, for R&R, and for hospital services to returning service personnel. Miami Beach reported some 140 hotels in military use. St. Petersburg had over 8,000 hotel rooms taken over by the Air Force Replacement Training Center Command, Boca Raton's unique radar training center. Service personnel found themselves stacked five or six deep in iron bunks in $100-a-day luxury suites.

The Army Air Corps built airfields all over the state. A generation later, private pilots would find tiny grass landing strips, often every twenty miles or so, along well-travelled routes, which had been used in training young pilots in the 1940s. Florida's weather cooperated greatly in the war effort, producing only about twenty nonflying days a year that would hamper training flights.

With B-17 bombers based at MacDill Field in Tampa, kids would see skies literally black with planes in formation, heading to war theaters around the world. It was routine for youngsters, hearing the drone of many engines, to stand, look up, gape-mouthed, and try to count the mighty B-17s.

In the Boca Raton area, which became the leading training center for America's new supersecret "radar" equipment, the air base eventually grew to over seventeen thousand men by 1945, with the base dwarfing the tiny town.

This same region saw the nation's first Civil Air Patrol Squadron, formed at Lantana Airport and used for search-and-rescue flights flown by civilians and veterans.

From a navy and merchant marine standpoint, from Pensacola to Key West, Florida's coastlines became a focal point for the services. In the Tampa area, nearly every able-bodied man not in service migrated to the city's shipyards, with the yards working around the clock, seven days a week. Workers gazed, fascinated, at paychecks soaring to $100-$175 per week—for ten-hour, seven-day workweeks.

Since virtually all vessels had been ordered to the Pacific theater, there were few craft to guard the hundreds of miles of Florida's Gulf Coast. It was said in many coastal areas that few available craft could have caught up with the slowest of German U-boats. The 500-tonners, which could crash-dive in seconds, carried fuel for a forty-two-day cruise, roaming Florida's coasts almost at will. The U-boats carried fourteen torpedoes, and deckguns able to sink most merchant ships from shellfire alone. Atlantic coastal eye witnesses tell of U-boat captains boldly surfacing in broad daylight, with sailors on deck taking snapshots, or even movies, of their sinking prey.

With tankers being hit and burning within sight of shore along the lower east coast, residents and children would rush to the beaches to view the scene.

Between 1942 and 1944, along the entire Atlantic seaboard, Florida coastal defenses sank only six German subs, while the Germans were launching an estimated one sub per day in the same period. In the highest loss month, May of 1942, eighty-six vessels were sunk off Florida's coasts, with only six Nazi subs known to be operating in the theater at the time.

The captain of the first U-boat to be captured, *U-128*, reported his subs were often sinking one ship per day, some visible from shore, as Nazi wolf packs roamed Florida's coasts, picking off freighters at random. During that May 1942, seven ships were sent to the bottom in one six-day period, with subs surfacing to finish off their prey with shellfire, thus saving torpedoes.

In the next month, June 1942, a "killer pack" of six Coast Guard cutters sank one sub near Key West.

All Florida must honor the valiant Coast Guard, with their unarmed patrol planes, tracking the Sea Wolves of the touted German Navy; as well as the Civil Air Patrol, spotter planes and Coast Guard crews who rescued downed airmen and seamen off Florida's coasts. Such rescues of crews from sinking, burning vessels were often unknown to the rest of the nation, buried under tons of releases from other theaters of the war around the world.

GOING WHERE MILLIONS OF PEOPLE
HAVE GONE BEFORE

And so, in our Florida time warp, we've touched down on some two hundred towns, villages, hamlets, and just plain places. We've viewed countless feats of valor, new things, and new excitement by dynamic dreamers and doers who've helped create those two hundred places. We've visited the haunts of Tristan de Luna, Menendez, deNarvaez, de Soto, Ponce, and old Juan Ortiz in our basket of history. We've checked over a hundred examples of things and stuff that maybe wouldn't have happened had there never been a La Florida; things and stuff that helped crackers become Crackers.

We've even covered a few true-falses of Things We Thought We Knew Till Now: absolute historical facts; our famous pirate, Gaspar; Capt. John Smith and Pocahontas; the name of America herself. These little numbers will come in handy someday, you'll see. You'll be glad you got 'em.

We've caught a glimpse of the continent that might have been: the United States of Florida. Of course, it's all in the eye of the beholder.

If you think we missed some favorite character of yours, be not dismayed. It will probably turn up in "The People" or "Empire Builders" chapters, just ahead. The treasure-seekers of the Great Plate Fleet of 1715 will be recreated in the Binder Boys in the land boom of the 1920s.

Historians tell us that the good old days were the greatest. Futurists tell us that the world of tomorrow will be Utopian. It is just this area in between that gives us problems. Oceanographers tell us that man can live for eons at the bottom of the sea. Space scientists tell us that man can exist for centuries, frozen in space. It is just this area in between that creates so much concern.

In this chapter, two facts come shining through. First, all things do cycle. That which has happened before in the past will probably happen again sometime in the future. And second, to see Florida tomorrow, we need only look to Florida yesterday and we will find our "tomorrows" are really up to us in our Florida of today.

This is one of the great lessons of history.

CHAPTER 4

The People

WE SET THE SCENE

It is not really just land that makes anyplace someplace. It is people!

In our people chapter, we'll visit Cubans of Tampa, Greeks of Tarpon Springs, Latins, the old Crackers, blacks, whites, ancestors of ancient Red Men, retired Midwesterners, New Yorkers, even Lafayette and his role in setting off Florida's first real land boom. We'll meet movers and shakers and just plain folks.

Florida is a mixture of the newly arrived and the old families. They're all a part of the 13 million Crackers of today's Florida: the folks at the Folk Festival in White Springs on the Suwannee River, the Cubans producing 25 percent of all cigars in America, the Vietnamese at Eglin Field, the new Haitian immigrants, and the daily arrival of new Crackers from all points north in the U.S.

The newly arrived bring with them an exciting challenge for Florida. As the population keeps growing, the land doesn't. Beginning in the 1700s, Florida was doubling her population every couple of decades.

In the 1780s, population was estimated at some 6,000 persons. By 1790, over 12,000 had found her. By the 1850s, the number soared to over 60,000, and by the 1870s, estimates ranged to the 300,000-400,000 mark, climbing to 500,000 by 1880, 800,000 by 1890, and 1,000,000 by the turn of the 1900s.

After the madness and mayhem of Florida's land boom of the 1920s, followed by the great depression, Florida's population remained static until 1940, when still with only about a million Crackers, she began the old doubling game all over again. From about one million people in 1940 (the twenty-seventh state in population), she grew to two million by 1950, four million by 1960, approaching seven million by 1970, and finally reaching thirteen million by 1990. While these numbers are intentionally general, they are specific enough to reflect the scenario, as every new Cracker who came in — say — 1960 will tell you!

By the mid-1970s, some areas were growing up to 10 percent per year. This meant a new neighbor for every ten on your street, every year!

With this influx, the deep south of Florida became very Northern in attitudes, while old North Florida became more and more "Old South." By the 1980s, Florida's legislature included only fifteen native Crackers, with the rest of the body from out of state.

Among the groups came the empire builders. The names ring a familiar bell, as well they should. Over a hundred names from America's industrial might came, bringing their fortunes with them . . . names that had been a part of America's culture ever since Americans first bought a saw or hammer, a car, or turned on a light bulb. We'll meet them in "The Empire Builders" chapter, just ahead.

It all began with the land. But it grew with the people: people who could virtually see into the future and rewrite the past; people who bought land and people who bought legislatures; people who gambled big and won dazzling gains; people who gambled big and saw their dreams go sour and crash on the rocks. Just ahead, we'll take you on a brief tour to meet a few of the more well known Titans. Then we'll meet more of the just plain folks who've really made Florida the Magic Land. We hope you enjoy the trip.

YOUR NEXT FLORIDA ABCs

Let's have a little exercise, now, on the people of Florida. In our drill, we'll give you a "clue letter" and tell you whether it is the first or last name of some of our Florida folks, plus a clue or two, just to help you out. The little dashes will even tell you how many letters there are in the name. You cross-word fans should have a field day with these. (If we miss a letter, like *X* or *Z*, it means we just couldn't come up with anybody. We'll make it up to you later on.)

You'll find all the names within this section, but again, among real Crackers, these folks are grade-school stuff. By the way, let's settle, once and for all, the Cracker question. We love you, Georgia, but "Cracker" really belongs to Florida, just like grits. Remember, Florida goes 'way back to 1513, and Georgia folks didn't start coming to these shores till about two hundred years or so later. As the old Cracker says, "We learn something new every single day, unless we're very, very careful."

A is for A _ _ _ _ _ _ , John James: Famed naturalist and bird watcher. Spent years writing of nature in Florida. Mr. Bok helped found society bearing his name. (Now see, that wasn't so difficult, was it?)

B is for B _ _ _ _ _ , Red: Famed sportscaster from Sanford. Started his announcing career on WRUF at University of Florida. He always said, "Just a-settin' in the catbird seat." (We're starting you out easy.)

C is for C _ _ _ _ _ _ , William D.: The "other rail-roader" who drove his rails west to Pensacola, founding town near there that bears his name.

D is for D _ _ _ _ _ _ _ , Hamilton D.: Of the great "saw family" fortune from Philadelphia. Made largest land buy in history: 4 million acres. Wanted to drain the Everglades. What a guy!

E is for E _ _ _ _ _ _ , Thomas: World's greatest inventor. Also an adopted Cracker in Ft. Myers. Workshop and home attract visitors today.

F is for F _ _ _ _ _ _ _ , Henry: King of all empire builders. Helped create two major cities, countless towns, and a railroad that went to sea, none of which bear his name.

G is for G _ _ _ _ _, Jonathan: Secretary of state after Civil War. Educated at Dartmouth and Princeton. Preacher, carpenter, founder of schools, state school superintendent. He did all this before his death at age forty-eight. A formerly all-black high school in St. Petersburg bears his name.

H is for H _ _ _ _ _ _ _ _ _, Papa: Keys' most famous resident, writer, and drinker. Adopted Cracker.

J is for J _ _ _ _ _ _, Tony: Flew very first commercial airliner, with one passenger on board, from St. Pete to Tampa.

K is for K _ _ _ _ _ _ _, John: One of Florida's most famous presidents. The Cape got named (temporarily) for him.

L is for L _ _ _ _ _ _ _ _ _, Marquis de: Was given huge tract of land anywhere he chose, for his help in Revolutionary War. Chose Florida.

M is for M _ _ _ _ _: Either one. Both built Palm Beach and Boca Raton in "their own image," larger than life (name both brothers for extra points and your initials in gold; in case of duplicates, ties will be awarded). (We'll get to the third brother later.)

N is for N _ _ _ _ _ _ _, Jack: Superstar who chose Palm Beaches for his home. Has a mini-golf course in his backyard, designed by him, of course.

O is for O _ _ _, Ransom E.: Great car-maker. Always wanted a town named after him, so he bought the land and built one.

P is for P _ _ _ _: The "Other Henry." Drove his rails down the Gulf Coast. Founded town which does bear his name. Also a high school in Tampa named after him.

Q is for Q _ _ _ _ _ A _ _ _ _'S W _ _: War in Europe bears this lady's name and title; British attacked St. Augustine. Couldn't take the fort. Nobody ever took the fort. (*Q* was a tough letter.)

R is for R _ _ _ _ _ _ _ _ _ _ _, John D.: World's richest man. Adopted Ormond Beach for his golf and to be near his friend (back under *F*). Famous for his dime tips.

S is for S _ _ _ _ _ _, Paris: Of the famed sewing machine family. Helped his *M* friend develop Palm Beach and Boca Raton. Also his own island bears his name today.

T is for T _ _ _ _ _ _, Zachary: Only commander ever to

defeat Seminoles in a battle. U.S. president in 1848. Wife's daddy was also president of the Confederacy.

V is for V _ _ _ _ _ _ _ _ (last name): Famous Italian navigator who explored Florida's Atlantic coast in the 1520s. "Narrows" bridge up north in New York City named for him.

W is for W _ _ _ _ _ _ (first name): Young English journalist who reported on Spanish-American War from Tampa as foreign correspondent. Got big job in British government later in WWII.

Y is for Y _ _ _ _, Joseph: Created his dream city on Gold Coast, named after the movie capital of the world. Planned it as an East Coast movie center.

Z is for Z _ _ _ _ _ _ _ : World-famous Babe. Florida superstar in golf and track and field events.

We'll give you one extra as a "no-points" bonus question.

W—is for: W _ _ _ _ _ _ _ _, W _ _ _ _ _ : She came within an ace of being queen, when the king gave up his throne for her. Once hostessed and waited tables in a rustic old inn in South Florida.

There you have just a few of the hundreds of powerful Florida people who left their mark on the state's lands, towns, and subsequent generations. Just ahead, before we get to the empire builders and Florida's incredible land boom, we'll meet some very special people who really didn't fit into any convenient category, for which we should all be grateful . . . for Florida would have been a different and a lesser place without them.

Many names will come up, bearing out the fact that virtually in no other instance in America have so many vitally interested movers and shakers poured energies and fortunes into a single mold, and brought about so much incredible change, as with Florida from 1490 to now. And it's only the beginning.

HOW DID YOU DO?

We know you got Audubon. Red Barber is the sportscaster we're looking for. William D. Chipley is the "other railroader" in the Panhandle. And Hamilton D. Disston, who came from a great Philadelphia saw-manufacturing family, is the big name we wanted.

Thomas Edison and Henry Flagler are, of course, the next names, and then comes Jonathan Gibbs, suave, urbane leader, minister, educator, and Florida secretary of state who died at age forty-eight, with Florida losing his incredible potential. Gibbs High School, a one-time all-black school in St. Petersburg, commemorates his name.

Then we have Papa Hemingway, otherwise known as Ernest. We know you got that. But how about Tony Jannus? In 1914 he was the pilot of this famous flight, along with one passenger, A. C. Pheil, mayor of St. Petersburg. (The plane only carried two people, and one had to drive.) Pheil had invested $500 in a raffle to win the honor of being the world's very first commercial airline passenger.

Of course you got Kennedy, and hopefully Lafayette too. He sold chunks of his unseen Florida land to, among others, a nephew of Napoleon, Achille Murat, whose descendants live today on parts of the original grant in the Tallahassee area.

The Palm Beach and Boca Raton brothers were Addison and Wilson Mizner.

We know you got Jack Nicklaus, but how about Ransom Olds? We ended up with some easier ones: Henry Plant, Queen Anne's War, John D. Rockefeller, Paris Singer, Zachary Taylor, Verrazano, Winston Churchill, Joseph Young, Babe Zaharias, and Wallis Warfield.

FROM THE GARDEN OF EDEN
TO PALM BEACH, WITH A FEW STOPS
IN BETWEEN

There are some people who simply did not fit into any convenient category, thank heavens. One of the real and rare Florida treasures is E. E. Callaway, little known except to history buffs. He was a lawyer, politician, and civic leader who spent his entire life trying to prove one single premise: the Garden of Eden was located in Florida, and not just in Florida, but in his own, personal hometown of Blountstown in West Florida (or Panhandle, if you prefer).

Callaway said that Noah built his ark in Blountstown, that

the biblical accounts are full of holes, and that the Garden of
Eden was not in Asia, or anywhere else, except Blountstown,
Florida. It was the straightforward Cracker mind-set at work.
During his lifetime, E. E. used scientific data to cite the location as the only spot on Earth with a four-headed river as de-
scribed in the Bible. He named the rivers, which combined to
form the Chattahoochee near Blountstown. He cited Bible
verse referring to "every tree pleasant to the sight, including
the sturdy gopher-wood tree, from which the ark was made,"
and claimed that all were in the area. He also saw fossil examples from limestone and riverbeds as proof that every species of life in the ark also existed in that area. In his lifetime,
he tried to prove the existence of 250 biblical plants, even the
much-maligned water-hyacinth plant, in Blountstown. (See
below about Mrs. Fuller from Palatka. She may have other
ideas.)

No promoter could ever do more for Florida, or for the
Garden of Eden, than E. E. Callaway. He was the granddaddy
of them all among devoted Florida Crackers and boosters. E.
E. Callaway, wherever you are, we salute you!

No less a zealot, though in a far more secular vein, is legendary J. E. ("Doc") Webb, merchant prince, promoter, genius, both loved and hated by customers and competitors in
St. Petersburg of the 1930s and 1940s. He was the creator of
"The World's Most Unusual Drugstore."

Webb's Drugstore, later Webb's City, sold shirts at half-
price, dollar bills for ninety-five cents, a six-cent breakfast,
and occasionally a three-cent breakfast. Depression families
poured into Webb's Cafeteria to line up on Sunday mornings
and buy breakfast for a whole family—two or three kids—for
under fifty cents total. But old Doc Webb got the folks downtown and into his World's Most Unusual Drugstore.

Webb even developed a "roofless cabaret," rococo-trimmed
pseudo-Spanish villa on the site of an old icehouse across the
street from his main buildings, along the railroad tracks. The
tracks separated the oldest black section from the rest of
downtown St. Pete; the choice of location itself was considered quite mad by other merchants. Nonetheless, Webb's
Cabaret featured the local high school dance band, playing
for fifty cents for folks who "danced under the stars" (on a
clear evening). The sheer excitement can only be imagined,

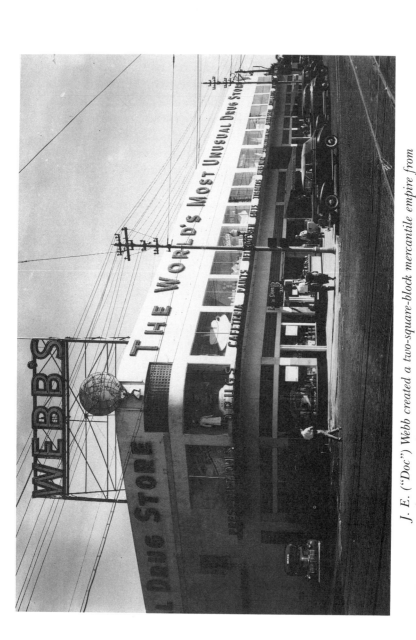

J. E. ("Doc") Webb created a two-square-block mercantile empire from a tiny, corner drugstore, as Florida crept through the depression days of the 1930s. (Courtesy St. Petersburg Historical Society)

unless you can share with the author his vantage point in the back row of the kid-trumpet section of the little dance band on those intoxicatingly clear Florida nights . . . especially when the trains didn't drown out the band. It was old Florida at its most hokey. And warmest.

Among some merchants, Webb was less than popular, possibly due to his genius at drawing attention to his own store. And genius it was. He garnered space in national press—*Life, Look, Colliers, Liberty,* and others did stories on the brilliant drugstore man from St. Pete.

Regardless of the merchants, his customers loved it! He was the symbol of recovery from the depression. Kids looked forward to—someday—working behind the nearly hundred-foot long super-soda fountain in the main store, where his most famous fountain concoction was a vertical banana split . . . banana slices upright in a tall, heavy soda glass, floating in three kinds of ice cream, three kinds of topping, coated with chocolate syrup, hot fudge, whipped cream, and nuts, with a cherry on top of the whole mess. It was the grandest, most expensive item on the whole fountain, and it cost an entire quarter! Webb's infamous "Banana Royale"—heaven could know no greater nectar.

At one point, Webb took out a two-page ad in the newspaper saying he needed $200,000 to expand his store. Within thirty hours, the entire issue of preferred stock was subscribed to by store patrons. But by the 1970s, with Webb having sold out and retired, his entire empire folded. With its passing came the end of an era in old St. Pete, the "turf" of one of Florida's most unusual people.

While all Florida people are not as high profile as the Garden of Eden fella, all played a role in creating our Florida of today. Consider the good doctor John Gorrie. Quickly now, a show of hands . . . how many recognize Doctor John's name? Be honest now.

Gorrie, considering his feats, has to be the unsung hero of the South. While searching for a malaria cure in Apalachicola, Gorrie accidentally began making what only Mother Nature had previously provided. What Benjamin Franklin's stove was to the North, Dr. Gorrie's creation was to the South. No single item has so affected Southern life, before or since. Few inventions have affected people the world over as has Dr.

Gorrie's uncredited feat. For Dr. Gorrie developed a method of making ice! This led to the world's first air conditioner, changing life forever in the South. It was 1848. Other patents preceded Gorrie's on the device, and the doctor died in 1855, with none of the recognition and rewards he deserved.

The names roll on, the wealthy, powerful, extraordinary, and ordinary folks. Among Florida's many "land boomlets" was the Pinellas County surge of 1911, as the county first became separated from Hillsborough County across the Bay. And, within the decade, "Dad" Gandy had completed his famed Gandy Bridge, linking downtown Tampa to St. Pete and generating a major land boom on the peninsula itself and on the approaches to the new bridge.

In the arts we have the famous "Yankee Lady," tiny, dynamic Harriet Beecher Stowe, settling in the hamlet of Mandarin on her orange-grove land, where she did much of her writing. Along with Stowe, the arts brought famed composer Frederic Delius, sent by his family from their home in Bradford, England to manage family lands in Florida (and to try to get the young man to lose his "crazy notion" of writing music). Delius promptly fell in love with Florida, composing his elegant "Florida Scenes" and "Florida Suite," finding the area even more stimulating, culturally, than his native England.

Even Ralph Waldo Emerson, in 1827, left his Massachusetts haunts and his famed Wayside Inn, to come to Florida to regain his health. And authoress Marjorie Kinnan Rawlings spent much of her life in tiny Micanopy, just south of Gainesville, amid tall pines and live oak; the setting for her novel *The Yearling,* and site for much of the filming of the resulting motion picture.

As the people kept a-coming, the international flavor grew. Danes founded White City in 1893. Swedes came in 1870 at the behest of Henry Sanford, former ambassador to Belgium, who had bought 12,000 acres, laid out a town, and named it—what else?—Sanford. Sanford was to struggle for its very existence. Within its first few seasons, it suffered a major town fire, quickly followed by a yellow fever epidemic. Just as quickly, the Great Freeze of 1893-94 destroyed much of its citrus crop, and much of the town.

Presidents make up an illustrious group in our look at the people of Florida. Many chief executives have adopted a special part of Florida to call their own. Grover Cleveland, with his colleagues, helped develop Green Cove Springs. His buddies included Mr. Lynch, who had opened a small brokerage firm; Gail Borden, who had a dairy farm; Mr. Hoover, who had just developed a thing called a vacuum cleaner; and a fella named J. C. Penney. Green Cove Springs never lacked for "angels."

We also have Teddy Roosevelt, with his troops in Tampa in 1897. Harry Truman's Key West Winter White House belongs on the roster, as does the JFK family compound in Palm Beach, where President Kennedy spent much of his youth. The list of the presidential contenders who didn't make it include the silver-tongued orator himself, William Jennings Bryan, major mover in the 1920s land boom; Alf Landon, a Florida fixture in the 1920s; and Adlai Stevenson.

Even George Washington played a supporting role in Florida's destiny. Following the Revolutionary War, President Washington helped arrange for that massive grant of land to his friend, the Marquis de Lafayette, in gratitude for his assistance during the war.

The world of incredible Cracker characters rolls on.

Ossian B. Hart of Ft. Pierce was the first—and almost only—Republican governor of Florida, 1873-77. Since 1513 (that's 350 years) there had not been a Republican governor, and it was to be almost another hundred years before the second one, Claude Kirk, in 1968. As our old "Bought-Legislature-Granddaddy" used to say, "I belong to no organized political party. I'm a Republican."

Josiah Walls, born a free black, rose to become—in 1883—the largest vegetable grower in the state, owning nearly two thousand acres of land. He served two terms in the Florida legislature and three terms in the U.S. Congress.

On the lower southeast coast, in 1885, the Postal Service created a very special mail route, hiring a mailman to walk the sixty miles from Lake Worth to Biscayne Bay. The mailman walked the hard, damp sand along the beach . . . and to save his shoes, he walked barefoot. Ted Pratt called it "the barefoot mailman route" in his 1943 novel, *The Barefoot Mailman.*

A Mr. Edwin Bradley and his sons had the $600-per-year contract. Each week they would start from Lake Worth and walk to the Orange Grove House of Refuge (later Delray Beach) the first night. The next day's walk covered twenty-five miles to the New River Refuge House in present-day Ft. Lauderdale. The third day's walk covered the last ten miles to Biscayne Bay, then by boat to the tiny Ft. Dallas terminus. At times, Bradley would take along "foot passengers," charging them five dollars to walk along with him.

By 1887, the Bradleys had retired, and in 1893, the service was ended as a road cut through the marshy wilderness and allowed wagons to carry passengers and freight to the new town at the south end of the sixty-mile route.

Mary McLeod Bethune, on her own initiative, with no funds at all, began a tiny school for disadvantaged black children, teaching them in her own home, begging for what supplies she might secure from whatever source. The lady did it all, many times completely alone, following her dream. The result is Bethune-Cookman College, now nationally recognized in Daytona Beach. Ms. Bethune opened her first school for girls in 1904, when she herself was still in her twenties. She also founded the National Council of Negro Women, and is honored by a seventeen-foot statue in Washington, D.C. She is totally unique among our Florida people.

Beginning in the 1890s, the tiny trading post of Linton began to take shape on Florida's southeast coast, partly from the impetus of Flagler's rails as they raced toward Miami. Some readers may learn here for the first time of an even earlier name for the town—that of Zion, then to become Linton, then Delray, and finally Delray Beach.

As rails brought prosperity and settlers, Flagler brought in many Japanese workers for his projects, providing housing and special rail rates for those who wished to ship crops to market. By 1907, hundreds came, until a separate town grew between present-day Delray Beach and Boca Raton. Settlers farmed, growing rice, tobacco, and pineapples, and worked the rails. Flagler even provided a special rail stop on the FEC, and later a U.S. post office for the town, given the name Yamato (an ancient word meaning Old Japan).

Eventually, Cuban competition hurt the pineapple market, and only a few of the original settlers remained: American-educated George Sakowan, who had helped establish the town, and George Morikami, who later farmed many, many acres. Morikami donated 140 acres of beautiful, wooded land southwest of Delray Beach to be dedicated to Japanese culture. Today, it is a memorial to the transglobal migration of the Japanese pioneers into Florida's history. It is Morikami Park. Yamato Road takes you there.

And the list continues. Dave Yulee was the son of the grand vizier to the sultan of Morocco and of Rachel Levy, daughter of a Jewish physician from England. Yulee became Florida's first U.S. senator, and as the creator of Florida's first cross-state railroad, he was the state's first millionaire. Yulee's life was so improbable as to be unsuitable even for fiction.

Yulee's father was born in a Moroccan harem. Yulee even arranged for the Florida legislature to effect a legal name change for him, naming himself David Levy Yulee after his two grandfathers. Eventually he was the owner of a 5,000-acre plantation at Homosassa Springs, and his name lives on in the town of Yulee and the county of Levy.

John Roebling, developer of tanks in World War II and grandson of the builder of the Brooklyn Bridge, built a huge compound near Sebring in 1926. In the hurricane of that year, he converted his entire holdings into a vast relief center for storm refugees. Later, the Roebling dream faded and little else was heard from his interests.

When H. Waldo Sexton, the Vero Beach creator of The Driftwood Inn and "Vero's Mountain," was asked why he built the mountain, he said, "'Cause I wanted to."

There's Dr. Henry Perrine, physicist and botanist, who developed his plant laboratory in the Keys, finally losing his life in the Indian Key massacre. Thanks to him, Florida introduced the lime, new lemons, and the avocado to the continent.

And Harris Mullen, having sold his *Florida Trend,* one of the South's leading publications, became a mover in the restoration of Ybor City, in Old Tampa. It will someday become a major, restored section of the city.

Then there's Dr. Odet Phillippe, adopted Cracker and one of the original settlers of the North Tampa Bay area, and poet Sidney Lanier, who began his career writing tourist pamphlets in North Florida. The trail is long and winding.

There's the blazing ninety-second "Welcome to Pensacola"—the world's shortest speech—by Mayor Vince Whibbs, a one-of-a-kind Cracker whizbang if there ever was one, and pride of America's "first place settlement."

Jacqueline Cochran, famed woman pilot, founded the WASPS—Women's Air Force Service Pilots—in World War II, and held hundreds of awards in aviation. Gen. Daniel ("Chappie") James was a one-time commander at Eglin Field, the largest U.S. Air Force base in the world. He was also the first black four-star general in American history; commander of NORAD and MAC, and a veteran of fighter missions in Korea and Vietnam . . . a towering leader during his lifetime. Pensacola can be proud to have added these two people to the state's honor roll.

Edward W. Bok was a founder of The Audubon Society. Bok Tower—or "Singing Tower"—is the highest point in Florida, placed atop Iron Mountain, which is 324 feet in height. With the tower adding over 200 more feet, the total height becomes almost 600 feet above sea level. In Florida, that's a mountain. It is said that, from its peak, one can see—if not forever—some 10 million oranges in every direction (or was it 10 billion?). And in this region, where one doesn't see oranges, one sees theme parks in the Theme Park Capital of the World (probably 10 billion).

The names continue to flow. From Governor Napoleon Bonaparte Broward, another Duval County governor (Jacksonville was eventually to claim eleven governors of the state), to Barron Collier and his empire, to the legendary Marjory Stoneman Douglas and her writings of the Everglades, to the contemporary Perry Como—Chris Evert—Jack Nicklaus—Pat Sumerall—Arnold Palmer—Ray Charles—Jackie Gleason—Burt Reynolds team, Florida's people continue to bring goodwill to their native or adopted land.

We are especially indebted to Rodney Allen for his fine, pictorial research in his work *Fifty-Five Famous Floridians*.

MRS. FULLER GOES TO THE PLANT FAIR

Another of the least heralded among our Florida people has to be "the little old lady from Palatka," Mrs. W. F. Fuller, who deserves her place in the sun in one of two major Japanese import events in Florida. One was the entire town of Yamato—and two, Mrs. Fuller's Incredible, Japanese Import.

In 1884, Mrs. Fuller of Palatka visited the Pan American Exposition in New Orleans. In the exotic-plant display, she spied a lively, purple flower from Japan. She brought a few of the blossoms home with her, placing them in her lily pond alongside the mighty St. Johns River.

To her astonishment, within a few days, the pretty plants had covered the entire lily pond, so she cleaned them out, tossing a few plants into the river flowing by her property.

Within a few days, she realized that the remaining plans had again filled her lily pond. She cleaned them out again, giving some to her neighbors and throwing the rest into the river.

Within a few more days, the entire banks of the river were covered with the incredible, purple blossoming plant. Mrs. Fuller even gave the plant a name, the St. Johns hyacinth.

By the mid-1890s, the St. Johns hyacinth had floated southward into the Kissimmee River, and was being considered by cattlemen to be used as cattle fodder. However, it was found the plant was 96 percent water, and cattle feeding on the plant could literally starve to death.

The plants continued to spread through rivers, streams, canals, all the way to the Everglades, filling virtually every body of water bank to bank. Its mesh was so strong, even alligators could not get through some of the tightly packed masses of purple flowers. The plant, being a Japanese import, had no nemesis in Florida. It had no natural place in the Florida food chain.

Near Belle Glade, two young lads, sons of lock tenders, actually hopped down from canal banks and walked on top of the hyacinths to dislodge a small trapped boat. They literally shoved the boat across the mass of plants, boys, boat, and all.

In the Everglades, near the end of World War II, an engineer, Lamar Johnson, viewing the problem, envisioned a special kind of wheel that might float *and* roll on top of the plants. It would be an amphibious "cruiser," letting its driver give the plants a spray-treatment to control its growth.

Johnson noticed, at a construction site, some huge cable spools, six to eight feet in diameter. Envisioning the spools as wheels, Johnson, through methods best known to him and his buddies at the construction site, secured four of the spools. He then found a four-wheel army surplus ammunition carrier in a Miami junkyard. Adding small motors and a steering platform, he attached giant air bags to the spools, and mounted them to the Rube Goldberg apparatus.

Astonishingly, the vehicle got the job done. It literally walked on water. Its giant spools, encased in the air bags, propelled the monster slowly over the tops of the hyacinth mass.

It had to have a name. It was a totally unique, first-time-ever vehicle, which walked on water. Johnson and his buddies conferred at length to come up with a moniker for the monster. The name finally given the vehicle came directly from the old Cracker mind-set. They named it: Jesus-Shoes!

Mrs. Fuller had no idea she had unleashed the famed Florida water hyacinth, which would "infect" Florida's waters for generations, resulting in millions of dollars being invested annually, simply trying to control the plant, let alone eradicate it. By 1949, some ten million dollars per year were being spent on hyacinth control. The incredible plant could reproduce itself every seventeen to thirty-seven hours.

By the 1990s, 100 years after Mrs. Fuller's visit to the plant show, the invasion had finally been slowed.

WELCOME TO MIAMI, MR. FLAGLER

In southeast Florida, it is remarkable that more awareness does not exist of the persona of "The Mother of South Florida," Julia Tuttle. Mrs. Tuttle, as a young widow, turned her back on a life of comfort and ease in Cleveland, journeying into the wilds of South Florida and literally bringing Henry Flagler and his rails, hotels, and fortune to Miami. Without Mrs. Tuttle, all Florida history may have been changed.

The Great Freeze of 1893-94 destroyed up to one hundred million dollars in citrus throughout the state, except in southeast Florida, where the "freeze line" apparently stopped just south of Palm Beach, Flagler's headquarters at the time. During the freeze, Mrs. Tuttle, aware that Flagler intended to end his line sixty miles north of her community, sent a courier to him, bearing an orange blossom from one of her trees, and a note saying, "See, it's not cold down here." Apparently that touch, plus a gift of six to twelve hundred acres of land

Palm Beach society came to see and be seen. This is Flagler's new Breakers Hotel. The man in the white knickers is said to be Kermit Roosevelt, son of President Theodore Roosevelt. "Afro-mobiles," as they were labeled at this time, were large, wicker wheelchairs powered by blacks turning bicycle pedals. A cluster of these may be seen in the background. (Courtesy Florida State Photographic Archives)

As Flagler's rails and hotels drove to Miami, its society also came to see and be seen. A tradition at the Flamingo Hotel in 1932 was its lawn-and-garden parties and teas. (Courtesy Florida Department of Commerce/Tourism Division)

held by Mrs. Tuttle and a neighbor, Mr. Brickell, brought about Flagler's decision to continue his rails south.

The vision of Mrs. Tuttle, along with Brickell and Flagler, helped create Miami from 1896 on, as well as many smaller towns that grew along the rails: Lake Worth, Lantana, Boynton Beach, Delray Beach, Yamato, Boca Raton, Ft. Lauderdale, and Hallandale. As Flagler's rails came to Miami, many settlers had never seen a locomotive before.

At one time, the Charlotte and Northern Railroad (you remember, the Gasparilla people) sold a spur line—the Seaboard Airline Railroad—to a fella from Baltimore, S. Davies Warfield. Warfield was a dynamic fella with a hatful of dreams; among them, to run his line across the state to join Mr. Flagler in southeast Florida. Along the way, Mr. Warfield determined that the perfect spot for the rails to meet would be the north end of Lake Okeechobee, and thereby hangs a tale.

Warfield and his advisors chose a tiny settlement to be named Indiantown as the location of the rail merger. It was a haven for fishermen, hunters, and sportsmen, and Warfield felt it would become a major sports center. He built the charming Seminole Inn, with rustic, wide halls, towering windows, and high ceilings, to host his—and Flagler's—wealthy train passengers for hunting and fishing vacations. The future of the town, inn, and rails was bright.

Warfield even brought his niece down from Baltimore to help at the inn, as waitress and hostess in the dining room. The young woman was already familiar with Florida (and its young naval cadets), having become pregnant, married, and quickly divorced in Pensacola. And so, the Lady Who Would Be Queen of all England also played out a role waiting tables in the tiny hamlet of Indiantown at her uncle's hotel.

In yet another instance of England's royalty bringing color and flavor to rural Florida, the tiny town of Sutherland in northern Pinellas County was created by investors led by the nineteenth duke of Sutherland, cousin to the queen. This duke brought his fortune, title, and dreams to the backwater area near Crystal River. Similar to his later cousin, he forsook his heritage, lands, and holdings for the woman he loved, a Miss May Blair, for whom he built a clapboard mansion and planted lands, even building a tiny Episcopal church where they could be married.

This duke, however, as a great favorite of the queen, was welcomed back to England at any time. He finally returned with his bride, leaving his Florida interests in other hands. The town of Sutherland eventually became "Palm Harbor." That's not very English, but after all, it was during the land boom.

THE SAGA OF OLD LAKE CITY

Lake City is a fascinating place, a midsized, old Southern town. Many families are multigenerational—born, "raised up," and died there, never leaving the town.

Now, Lake City goes waaay back. It was called Alligator, and even before that it was the tiny ghost town of Corinth, founded by families migrating in from St. Marys, Georgia . . . the Cones, Browns, Deans, Sumeralls, Knights, Goodbreads, and others. The families produced several state legislators, an army chief-of-staff in Gen. C. P. Sumerall, a major TV sports star in Pat Sumerall, and a governor in Fred Cone. Marion S. Knight served in the state legislature of 1899, which turned out to be the famous (alleged) "bought" session, the one which produced the "Flagler Divorce Law."

In 1901, Knight's constituency back in Lake City did receive a handsome gymnasium from Flagler, said to represent some twenty thousand dollars. Town councilmen were reported to have reservations about the gift, coming, as it did, on the heels of the divorce law. But apparently someone voiced the council consensus, saying, "Well, the town does need a new gym."

Within five years, the town was to see its entire education-complex "simply moved away." Its main school, eventually known as the University of Florida, was moved to Gainesville, down the road. Among old-timers who remember hearing about the 1905 "move," sentiments are mixed to this day. But the gym served the town well for nearly a century, with several generations of kids playing basketball in its handsome interior.

But, back to the University of Florida story. The state superintendent of public instruction, William Holloway, before

The very old-time Lake City had a laid-back charm. At Blanche and Marion streets was the smallest hotel in town. (Courtesy Florida State Photographic Archives)

being named to the state office, had spent twelve years as head of Gainesville's schools. On getting the state position, he apparently began a campaign to persuade the state assembly to move the University of Florida to his town. With an eye toward diversifying state schools, the assembly finally introduced a bill.

The bill was to reorganize the state college system and create two universities; one for boys, east of the Suwannee River, and one for girls, west of the Suwannee (gotta keep the young ones moral after school). Then bidding began from towns wanting the schools. According to town records, Gainesville filed a bid for the "boys' school," offering some 517 acres of land, $40,000 in cash, use of its high school building, and free water.

Lake City pointed out that much investment had already been made in state dollars in the existing plant, plus the school was already holding some 871 acres, 350 more than was offered by its neighboring town. Lake City also offered its own certified check for $40,000 and stated it would provide free water, too, if that were to be a factor.

As local veterans tell it, in spite of the matching funds, 50 percent more land, and matching water, the school was simply "spirited away" and got moved down the road to Gainesville, with the Lake City plant closed. In legendary political moves, various schools were moved, changed, and consolidated, and the "new" University of Florida was begun in Gainesville.

The saga of the gender-divided schools continued into the 1940s, with the boys' school in Gainesville becoming the University of Florida, and the "girls' school" in Tallahassee becoming F.S.C.W.: Florida State College for Women. The first men to graduate from F.S.C.W. were in 1949, by which time the school was well established as Florida State University, with Gainesville having "gone co-ed" many years before.

One of Florida's treasures, Miss Lassie Goodbread Black, matriarch of the Goodbread clan in Lake City, was the first woman to enroll at the "boys' school" when it was made co-ed by law. Miss Lassie was also the first woman to graduate from the university, with a degree in agriculture.

Lake City was to be a major player in another part of Florida's history; that of the railroads. Now you newcomers, try to

listen up and follow along with us. The road will seem circu-
itous, but old Crackers will have no trouble at all in grasping
the logic, and even knowing the outcome. Remember, it all
leads somewhere. Trust us.

In 1851, the state sought rail companies to run a line from
Jacksonville to the town of Alligator, the original name of
Lake City. The State Board of Internal Improvements had
set aside a half-million acres of land for rail use. Two compa-
nies filed proposals: the Atlantic and Gulf, and the Florida
Railroad Company.

The state board planned to award rail interests some 200
feet of right-of-way for rails, and as a gift, alternate sections
of 640 acres—up to six miles wide on both sides of the rails.
In addition, bonds of up to ten thousand dollars per mile of
track would be issued for purchase of track and rolling stock,
such bonds to be secured by the state lands given to the investors by the state board. The lands were also pledged as security, in the event railroaders failed to live up to their
promises.

Lake City folk were urged by their leaders to buy the
bonds—if need be, "to bet the farm" to bring the railroad to
town. Which they did.

And speaking of following along at this point, it was astonishing to find the "total recall" of senior Crackers in the area,
who could remember "chapter and verse" of the Lake City
Rail Saga, even though versions and dollars would vary from
story to story. Lake City folks just don't forget.

The town voted a $100,000 bond issue, with proceeds to be
paid directly to the rail groups. In addition, the rails received
200,000 acres of state lands, 200,000 acres of federal lands,
$600,000 in guaranteed bonds (are you with us?), $50,000 in
city bonds (the ones bought by the "little people" who bet the
farm), and $100,000 in direct payment from the Columbia
County treasury. Noted historian Edward F. Keuchel has documented much of the business in his *History of Columbia
County,* along with the research of Ms. Nettie Black (Goodbread) Ozaki, a prime mover in the Keuchel book project.

Even with all this largesse, for two to four years virtually
nothing happened. The rails finally reached Lake City—
fourteen years later—after the bond issued by the town.

But wait. There's more. Now comes the good part for Old Crackers.

The Internal Improvements board, which dealt out all the above goodies to the competing rail lines, included two distinguished men, Stanley Baldwin and David Yulee. Baldwin was president of the Atlantic and Gulf Rails, and Yulee was president of the Florida Railroad Company.

We are indebted to Nettie Black Ozaki for her beautiful introduction to the Keuchel work. As she writes, "Although Columbia County is one of Florida's earliest communities, it has been one of the last to be written about. . . . When footpaths to Miami and Tampa were being hacked through the tall grasses, Lake City folks were already established . . . and when St. Petersburg was not a flicker in the night, Lake City was a town of well built homes with books and tall candles."

The fact that Lake City courthouse records were destroyed by fire not once, not twice, but three times and still the historical society could generate all its data speaks volumes of the dedication of Ms. Ozaki and all the members of the Columbia County Historical Society. This writer is proud to share family soil in the tiny Corinth Churchyard Cemetery with our mutual ancestors.

And we must also salute the incredible Lassie Goodbread Black, the lady whose contributions and accomplishments alone could have filled many of these Lake City pages, and the lady for whom the entire town turned out simply to say, "Happy birthday, Miss Lassie."

THE SAGA OF OLD TOM EDISON

Thomas Alva Edison was thirty-eight years old and sickly when his doctors told him he might die from his breathing problems. Tom moved to Florida and sure enough he died— forty-six years later, at age eighty-four.

Of his hundreds of inventions, one most often overlooked was his development of "prefab housing." Tom had his twin homes prefabricated in Maine and shipped to Ft. Myers to be assembled on his riverfront land. His good friend Henry Ford visited him often, so Tom gave one of the houses to Henry.

The two were soon joined by another crony, naturalist and writer John Burroughs, and still later, a fourth friend, Harvey Firestone, joined them and the old neighborhood was never the same. The foursome ran around together. Ford gave Edison a special, handmade Ford flivver with wide-track wheels, designed to match the ox-rut roads out in the country, so the cronies could go riding; thus probably creating the world's first wide-track car.

In a story that could only happen in these circumstances, the four men—the world's most famous inventor, the world's tire king, a famed naturalist/author, and the fabled automaker—were riding in the country and, as can only happen in a story such as this, had a flat tire. Along comes a service truck from—you guessed it—the local Firestone garage. A young man gets out of the truck and proceeds to change the tire for the four venerable gentlemen.

As he completes the job, one of the men in the flivver (you remember what a flivver is, don't you?) says, "Young man, I don't suppose you'd know this, but I am Harvey Firestone."

YOUNG MAN: "Suuure you are!"

FIRESTONE: "And this fella here is Henry Ford, and over here is John Burroughs."

YOUNG MAN: "Right!"

FIRESTONE: "And our driver is Thomas Edison."

YOUNG MAN: "Right. And I'm George Washington, and the guy in the truck is Abraham Lincoln."

Ft. Myers folks swear to it. And it is said the young man did receive a brand-new Ford flivver a little later, and the owner of the garage got a brand-new set of Firestones for his car. Leastwise, that's the way they tell it in Ft. Myers.

It's a good story, and probably at least partly true. We're indebted to Vernon Lamme, the Lamme estate, and the Lamme family for Vernon's firsthand account of the tale . . . and to Bill Beck of Star Publishing, who handles all the Lamme books, for his assistance.

Another Florida town boasting some big names was the unlikely hamlet of Green Cove Springs, tucked away from the mainstream of development, nestled near a slow bend in the mighty St. Johns River southwest of Jacksonville. World War II buffs will remember the town as one of the locations of Uncle Sam's "Mothball Fleet," as America stored rows of warships along the river wharves in the sleepy town. Green Cove Springs sprang from a whole fraternity of promoters. Mr. J. C. Penney was first, planning to develop a retirement village for ministers. He bought land, creating "Penney Farms." Soon, his friend, dairyman Gail Borden, came in on the plans, along with Hoover of vacuum cleaner fame. Then Mr. Lynch and Grover Cleveland joined the group.

With all this support, the town became a tourist mecca, with hotels, riverboats, inns, and health-giving spring waters. Soon after, Cleveland got a good job up in Washington, D.C. He used to have his buddies ship Green Cove Springs bottled water to the place where he worked, a place called the White House.

Still another product of this amazing town came about in the person of D. P. Davis, native son, destined to become a Cracker dynamo. Davis, a school dropout, got into construction work, then real estate. He saw folks dredging bay bottomlands in Biscayne Bay, turning it into gold. He was so fascinated that he moved to Tampa, secured permits, and—against much opposition—dredged the mudflats of Tampa Bay near downtown. He built seawalls, backfilled with sand, and was thrilled to find that he, too, had created land—saleable land! The result was Davis Islands, the hottest project in town.

While Davis is revisited in the "Empire Builders" chapter just ahead, suffice it to say that he sells nearly two million dollars in lots—downpayments only—rushes back to St. Augustine to repeat his accomplishments, and the land boom stumbles and dies. Davis loses his entire fortune, and is said to have hurled himself overboard on an ocean cruise.

THE IRLO BRONSON MYSTERY

Motorists on U.S. 192, passing through Kissimmee, will see small, blue and white highway signs, bearing the legend, "Irlo Bronson Memorial Highway." Eventually, someone will turn to a spouse and say, "Who do you suppose this Irlo Bronson person was?"

People will wonder this as they travel this land of every known go-cart thrill and every possible hole of miniature golf—this Global Center of Fun, carved, as it were, from a vast cow pasture in the heart of Florida (poetic, but true)! There are seas of campsites and hotel and motel rooms. In 1971, when Walt Disney World opened, there were said to be some thirty thousand hotel rooms under construction in the area all at the same time. The area around U.S. 192 has come to be known as "Maingate"—one word, like "damnyankee." The meaning? We'll give you a clue. It's very near the main gate of the world's most popular tourist destination, and we're talking *planet*! Got it? Good.

Now, back to the Irlo Bronson Memorial Highway. George Bronson, along with other cattle barons in the 1920s, spent time and money acquiring vast acres of wasteland for cattle grazing—some two hundred thousand acres of it. Following George's death, his son, Irlo, took over management of the cattle lands. (The story may be apocryphal, though provided repeatedly by historical societies, Chambers of Commerce, area hotel executives, and finance people who should know.)

Irlo was traveling over his lands one day when a realtor friend stopped him with a question.

FRIEND: "Hey, Irlo, how big's that 'piece' you got down there?"

IRLO: "Heck, I dunno, 'bout ten thousand acre, I guess."

FRIEND: "How much's it worth?"

IRLO: "Ain't worth nothin'. Tried to give it to the state while back. They turned it down."

FRIEND: "Got a guy give you a hunnerd an acre for it" (Cracker for $100 an acre).

IRLO (In lightning arithmetic, figures 100 times 10,000 has got to be a heavy load. Wa'nt none of his tars still in the sand.): "OK."

So the deal is set. This is the type of complicated, high-finance, old-Cracker litigation that went on in deep-pocket circles.

(You folks with heart conditions, watch out. This gets tense. They always said Irlo got right down to where the water hit the wheel! Wa'nt no weevils in his wheat! Maybe you just better skip the rest of this chapter.)

Anyway, at the deal's closing, it was found that some nine hundred acres of the land had a clouded title. Irlo's friend said, "We'll take it anyhow at the hunnerd. Get the title cleared on the rest, and we'll take it too at whatever the going rate is." The buyer, by the way, turned out to be some fella from out of state, not even a real Cracker. Humph! Wa'nt from Florida at all. Buyin' up all that good grazin' land to open some kind of amusement park. Well, I should say! Some people! Some of his jelly done fell off his cracker.

Irlo said, "OK." And set about doing it.

Well sir, by the time Irlo got the title cleared, months had gone by and the "going rate" had moved from "a hunnerd" to $3,707 an acre. Irlo's first 9,000 acres was said to be about a million dollars. The last 900 was said to be about $4 million dollars. Irlo Bronson became one of the first, if not the first, of many land-sellers in what was to become the foremost tourist destination on the planet. And that's who Irlo Bronson was.

But wait. There's more. Shortly after, there was said to be a cadre of some one hundred real-estate folks working for this buyer independently of one another, some without full knowledge of their client's identity. They acquired nearly twenty-eight thousand acres near sleepy old Kissimmee, a tract of land nearly one hunnerd times the size of this fella's amusement park out west, all at an average price of about $185 per acre, so the local folks said, over a five-year period during the 1960s. It was a far cry from old Hamilton Disston and his 4 million acres at 25 cents apiece.

There was also a "little old lady" who is supposed to have held on to a few acres, smack-dab in the middle of everything. Some folks say she still holds on to that little "piece."

With about twenty-eight thousand acres, and folks guessing it was about $185 an acre (nobody knew for right-sure), it would come to about $5.5 million for the whole piece, just 'cause this nice fella wanted to open an amusement park.

Well sir, all this came to a head about October 1971, when the buyer opened that amusement park, just like he said he was goin' to. And do you know? In 1990, about twenty years later, there was still one little old sixty-acre piece, just a-hanging loose out there. But this little piece borders on a whole bunch of big roads and a new beltway they're going to build around the town, borders a train station for another super-speed train, borders on a whole new movie park by some other Hollywood folks, and borders on even some more expansion by the original fella himself. (Of course he's gone now, but his company's going to do it anyway.) There are lots of folks laying claim to this piece, even some possible court trials coming up about who really owns the piece and even who gets the rights to buy it from each other and all sorts of goings on.

Talk about research! You can get months of notes just from the barbershop in Kissimmee or from every motel in the Theme Park Capital of the World. Everyone has his own version of what's going on.

Now how much do you figure this little old 60-acre piece is going to wind up costing, counting court costs, lawyers, agents, and all the rest, let alone the value of the land? You guessed it, about forty three million dollars, eight times the amount the entire 28,000 acres was said to have cost back in the 1960s. Now that's a land boom.

So now you know at least a few of our Florida people: from mighty presidents to just plain folks; from Mrs. Fuller's hyacinth pond to Doc Webb's world's most unusual drugstore, to E. E. Callaway's Garden of Eden. Just remember, virtually nowhere else have so many movers and shakers brought so much of their lives and fortunes to a single, giant gameboard as in Florida.

And the empire builders were just coming.

CHAPTER 5

Empire Builders

ROGUES, ROBBER BARONS, AND RAILROADERS

Somewhere in the land, as you read these lines, a group of investors is viewing a large wall map. A young man in a three-piece suit is tapping the map with a pointer. He speaks. "In this tract, J.B., we have 2,800 acres, which projects to 14,000 units. Sales will top off at $138 million, a seven-year net of 27.4 percent on equity, etc., etc." All are assured riches in the land of perpetual sunshine.

In the magic land of Florida, stories abound about the old empire builders, adopted Crackers buying land, buying legislatures, building dreams. Whether rogues, rascals, rapscallions, renegades, robber barons, or railroaders (some were none of the above), their names became legend: Flagler, Plant, Disston, Merrick, Davis, Ball, Snell, Warfield, Collier, DuPont, Fisher. Ahead we'll have some Florida ABCs for you to work on. These are just a few of them. These empire builders could virtually have their way with the early settlers who followed their leads, bought their land, and built their railroads, bridges, and cities. An old Cracker parson had a phrase for it. He used to say, "I wanna be around when the meek inherit the earth, so I can watch the unmeek take it away from 'em."

Each placed a personal stamp on Florida, helping bring her to her present-day family of 13 million Crackers. The old Cracker parson used to say these were the true Florida preachers. They were evangelists, preaching the gospel of Florida. Their names abound across the land on bridges, roads, counties, cities, towns, banks, even on a tree! Spanning a half-century, from 1880 to 1930, the Titans came to their new playing field to try their luck, bringing their fortunes with them.

We'll meet a whole crowd of these. And remember, all these events occurred in the days when there was no federal income tax, no social security, no FICA, no estate taxes, no personal taxes, and no sales tax. It's hard to imagine, but true. America's Titans of industry often amassed such hordes of dollars, they literally didn't know what to do with them. They brought a lot of 'em to Florida.

A is for A _ _ _ _ , John Jacob: The very first guest in Flagler's new Miami hotel checked in three days before it opened. He also founded a tiny town bearing his family name, sold it out, and left Florida, a rare occasion.

B is for B _ _ _ _ , William Jennings: Secretary of state under Wilson, real-estate promoter, and Sunday School teacher.

B is for B _ _ _ , Ed: Managed DuPont interests into another Florida fortune in lumber, paper, land, and banking.

B is for B _ _ _ _ _ _ : One of Miami's first retail families. The original Orange Bowl bore this name.

B is for B _ _ _ _ _ , Gail: Had giant dairy company. Joined his buddies in helping create Green Cove Springs.

B is for B _ _ , Edward W.: Created "Singing Tower," on highest point in state, near Lake Wales.

C is for C _ _ _ _ _ _ , William D.: The "other railroader" ran his rails west to Pensacola, and to the town bearing his name.

C is for C _ _ _ _ _ _ , Barron: Created virtual fiefdom, in county bearing his name. Was streetcar "carcards" tycoon in Baltimore and Washington.

C is for C _ _ : Media family from Ohio (newspapers, radio, TV, cable). One even ran for president once.

D is for D＿ ＿ ＿ ＿, D. P.: From Green Cove Springs. Created downtown islands bearing his name in Tampa. Lost entire fortune in land boom/bust.

D is for D＿ ＿ ＿ ＿, Arthur Vining: Brought his Alcoa fortune to Florida; was eighty-one when he arrived. Created another acronym and another fortune to go with it in Florida.

D is for D＿ P＿ ＿ ＿: Worldwide chemicals fortune. Its interests were managed so well in Florida by a son-in-law (*B*), that it made still another fortune and empire.

D is for D＿ L＿ ＿ ＿, Henry: Fabrics man created town bearing his name. Teamed with his "hat-man" friend to create major Florida university bearing "hat man's" name.

D is for D＿ ＿ ＿ ＿ ＿ ＿, James: Heir of famous tractor works. Created incredible estate on the bay in Miami, Vizcaya, with 20 million tractor dollars.

E is for E＿ ＿ ＿ ＿ ＿, Thomas A.: Famous inventor who adopted Florida and developed the Famous Foursome of Ft. Myers. These should be getting easy for you by now.

F is for F＿ ＿ ＿ ＿ ＿ ＿ ＿ ＿, Harvey: World's tire king. Became another of the Famous Foursome with his buddy, *E*.

F is for F＿ ＿ ＿, Henry: Another "Famous Foursome" member. Created handmade Tin Lizzie for his host in the Ft. Myers Foursome.

F is for F＿ ＿ ＿ ＿ ＿, Carl: Brought his car-racing fortune to Florida and created Miami Beach. At age fifty, he said he earned $1 million for every year of his life.

G is for G＿ ＿ ＿ ＿, Clarence: "Feudal baron" who took over the Boca Raton Hotel after the land crash. An Indiana reservoir bears his name (no, not the Clarence Reservoir).

K is for K＿ ＿ ＿ ＿ ＿: Along with the Wall family, this one created major Tampa hardware and mercantile interests.

K is for K＿ ＿ ＿ ＿ ＿: Along with the Ridder interests, created Florida newspaper empire, then national media giant (same as *K* just above, only another family).

L is for L＿ ＿ ＿ ＿ ＿, Scott: Sold gravel on his bike. Created Scotty's Stores from family materials firm. Should have been with us a lot longer.

M is for MacA＿ ＿ ＿ ＿ ＿, John D.: Brought insurance fortune to Florida; operated billions from a corner table in his hotel coffee shop.

M is for M _ _ _ _ _ _, George: Sparked land boom with his incredible Coral Gables town in Miami.

P is for P _ _ _ _, A. C.: Mayor of St. Petersburg, and very first paying airline passenger in the history of man — from St. Pete to Tampa.

P is for P _ _ _ _ _ _, J. C.: Had famous chain of stores. Started retirement farm for ministers with help from his friends. It became Green Cove Springs.

R is for R _ _ _ _ _ _ _ _, John: Circus king who brought his fortune to Florida and gave it to Sarasota.

S is for S _ _ _ _ _, Perry: A beautiful isle in St. Petersburg is named after him, as well as a downtown arcade filled with art and sculpture, gracing Old Central Avenue.

S is for S _ _ _ _ _: Media family whose empire included radio, TV, and cable in Ohio and Florida.

S is for S _ _ _ _ _ _ _, John B.: This "hat man" joined his friend Mr. "D" to develop a major university bearing his name. The law school is the former Rolyat Hotel from the land boom.

W is for W _ _ _ _ _ _ _ _, S. Davies: Ran his Seaboard rails across the state to join Flagler. Built Indiantown's Seminole Inn.

IT WAS DIRTY WORK,
BUT SOMEBODY HAD TO DO IT

It was the era of Goulds, Astors, Vanderbilts, and Morgans, who simply lived beyond the lives of kings. It was in this period that a certain "strain of person" began to discover Florida. Let's check out just a few of the major players.

Under *A*, one of the few times the Astor family ever *sold* anything was with their tiny settlement of Astor, in which the family lost interest and withdrew. The traditional Astor rule was "buy and hold; never sell." John Jacob was the first guest at Flagler's new Miami hotel, three days before it opened.

Under *B*, William Jennings Bryan was the combination Sunday School teacher and real-estate promoter, while Ed Ball was the successful DuPont manager.

B is also for the Burdine family, creating their mercantile dynasty of Burdines Stores throughout Florida, as well as

Roddy Burdine Stadium, destined to become the Orange Bowl in Miami.

And *B* must include Gail Borden, joining with his friend J. C. Penney to help create the town of Green Cove Springs. Edward W. Bok was the creator of famed Bok Tower, near Lake Wales.

That first *C* must be William Chipley, the "other rail-roader," who drove his rails west. Then we have Barron Collier, with his entire Collier County land. He comes up just ahead. And, of course, we have the Cox family, who brought their media interests from Ohio, creating another media empire in Florida.

Under *D,* we will have much to say about D. P. Davis, from Green Cove Springs, the firebrand who created Davis Islands in Tampa. The "other" Davis, Arthur Vining, and his Arvida Corporation come up later, also.

The DuPont family interests grew into still another Florida fortune in paper, lumber, and banking. And *D* also means Henry De Land, fabrics man from New York and Philadelphia who created the town of De Land, and along with his friend, "hat-man" John B. Stetson, created Stetson University there.

D is also for James Deering, of the McCormick/Deering farm equipment fortune, who built his incredible Vizcaya palace overlooking Biscayne Bay in Miami.

Continuing on, *E* is for Tom Edison, founder of the Famous Foursome of Ft. Myers. He is the world's greatest inventor and our most famous adopted Cracker.

The first *F* is Harvey Firestone, part of the Foursome in Ft. Myers. The next *F* is for Henry Ford, friend of Edison, who moved in with the Foursome. Still the other *F* is for Carl Fisher, who developed the Indianapolis 500 Mile Racetrack, and brought his fortune to Florida to "invent" Miami Beach.

Under *G,* the "feudal baron" who took over the bankrupt Boca Raton Hotel was Clarence Geist. Details on Geist are also just ahead.

We have Knight twice under *K* for the Knight-Wall firms of Tampa, early merchant successes, and the Knight-Ridder media dynasty encompassing the nation today.

This particular ABC is dedicated to the owner of this *L.* It stands for Scott Linder, who made his first sales call for

Linder Materials on a folding bicycle, before graduating to head the family firm and going on to create Scotty's Stores of Florida. He also helped create the Florida Council of 100, a group of corporate leaders across the state. Scotty, a true Cracker gentleman, didn't stay with us nearly long enough.

John D. MacArthur was the insurance magnate who operated his empire from his own hotel coffee shop on Singer Island, itself planned by that sewing machine fella, Paris Singer. And George Merrick virtually sparked the Miami portion of the land boom, with his Coral Gables development.

Now under *P*, St. Pete Mayor A. C. Pheil was the world's very first paying airline passenger. Another *P* was the fella who got all those guys together to help start Green Cove Springs, J. C. Penney.

By now you know the *R has* to be John Ringling, circus king, who left his mansion, his museum, his art, and all his holdings to his adopted hometown of Sarasota.

And in the *S* group, we'll start with Perry Snell, creator of beautiful Snell Isle in St. Petersburg, as well as the Snell Arcade downtown. The massive media empire has to be the Storer family from Ohio, and one more *S* belongs to John B. Stetson.

Finally, the *W* is for Mr. S. Davies Warfield, "the fourth railroader," who built the charming Seminole Inn, at Indiantown, planning to make the town his personal metropolis.

There you have some of the visionaries who created their own dreams, bringing a special spark to Florida, and most definitely *not* leaving Florida as they had found her.

On a tiny scale, even Menendez, who probably brought the first oranges to Florida from Spain, also brought pressures of change to the raw land he found in 1565.

From Citrus Tower, off U.S. 27 in Central Florida, one can see—if not forever—certainly oranges. Tens of billions of them sparkle against the green velvet of millions of orange trees. During blossom season, the fragrance from billions of orange blossoms fills the air, into your closed car as you drive through the area.

All this came from the original empire builder. He was working for the king of Spain at the time.

It just took a little longer for his work to show results. The empire builders 300 years later worked a bit more quickly.

FLORIDA'S TWO HENRYS

Florida had "two Henrys." They sort of paralleled each other, just as they sort of paralleled England's "two Henrys," King Henry I and King Henry II, a few generations earlier. Both sets of Henrys took vast regions of raw land and tiny groups of the "little people" and helped weld them into a dynamic culture, largely through sheer leadership and drive.

These two players—almost symbolically—chose opposite sides of the state for their creative urges. Their combined assets and commitments may only be guessed at in 1990 dollars, but the figure would certainly be in the billions.

We'll begin with Henry Plant, Connecticut Yankee, developer, and, chronologically, Henry the First.

Florida was on its way in the 1880s. Railroads would play a major role in her future. If the rails passed your town by, it was good-bye Charlie. Your town may as well close up shop. Check out the booming village of Magnolia. The trains had to go through your town, and hopefully, make a stop! You had to have a station, or you were Deadsville. And everybody knew it.

Connecticut Yankee Henry Plant had come south and entered the railway express business, shipping and billing freight on rail lines. That incredible development took place in the 1860s, when Confederate President Jefferson Davis approved a special dispensation allowing Plant to continue his freight service through the Civil War. Plant, a Northerner, not only kept his company, but prospered, serving Confederate troops. He was a Yankee under a special, protective arm of the Confederacy, the only such Yankee and, given the temper of the times, it was quite incredible.

Even more astonishingly, after the war, Plant was allowed to *keep* his company. Again, as far as research can show, he was the only Northerner so allowed. As one historian noted, this would be tantamount to Roosevelt, Churchill, and Stalin operating a munitions factory in downtown Berlin from 1940 to 1945. It was another world, another time.

Plant began to build his fortune, acquiring tiny, struggling rail lines that had been damaged during the war. By the 1880s, his rails reached down the Gulf Coast, as he planned a major port and city in the settlement of Cedar Key.

Upon finding that a sale contract did not include land or port facilities, Plant simply bypassed the settlement, moving on to Tampa, which welcomed him with open arms, and where he did develop a major port, rail terminus, steamship company, and eventually the legendary Tampa Bay Hotel, one of the most unusual buildings in Florida—then and now.

Plant was seventy-six years old when he opened his new Tampa Bay Hotel in 1891. Just a season later, he began plans for his Belleview Biltmore Hotel, helping create the town of Belleair, near Clearwater. Indeed, Plant opened his Belleview Biltmore in 1894, beating—by design—the opening of Henry Flagler's Royal Palm Hotel in Miami by one day. Today, the Belleview Mido, still a mind-boggling, Victorian, multigabled artifact sitting plumb in the middle of old Gulf-Coast Florida, remains a genuine Florida treasure. Plant's incredible Tampa Bay Hotel, minarets, parapets, Moorish rococo gables, and all, in 1991 celebrated its 100th birthday, as one of Florida's most remarkable buildings—and home of the University of Tampa.

As Plant brought his rails to town, Tampa citizens watched their village of some twelve hundred souls explode to a bustling city of over five thousand people. The rule of the rails had claimed another victim in the charming hamlet of Cedar Key, which was to see growth and progress—along with the rails—pass it by for nearly a century.

Plant died in 1899, having set a pattern for all empire builders to follow, including Flagler, who pursued a similar pattern down Florida's eastern seaboard.

Henry Plant accomplished one thing that eluded Flagler—a city bearing his name. There are Flagler Avenues, a Flagler Beach, Boulevard, banking chain, high school, even a college. Plant had most of those too. But there was no Flagler City.

THE FLAGLER SAGA UNFOLDS

Probably the most powerful of all the forces that were to help shape Florida was Henry Flagler. His name adorns roads, boulevards, beaches, banks, schools, yet the two or three cities he helped create, the Overseas Railroad, and the resulting Overseas Highway bear no testimony to Henry Flagler.

He created Palm Beach, and then created West Palm Beach for those who were to serve his Palm Beach residents.

He sparked the emergence of Miami. Even when Mrs. Tuttle was said to have offered to change the town's name to Flagler City, he modestly declined, leaving it with its old Indian name, Miami.

His Overseas Railroad no longer exists. The Overseas Highway built on its old roadbed is called simply U.S. 1. Even the street leading to the highway in Key West, to which Flagler brought the first train many natives had ever seen, is called "Harry Truman Boulevard."

Travelling down Florida's eastern seaboard, circa 1880s-1912, we meet Flagler all along the way. He began with rails and hotels in Jacksonville in 1883. Each time a cold spell would reach him, he would apply a few more Standard Oil millions and drive his rails southward to the next town.

The next town after Jacksonville was St. Augustine. He built three hotels here. Then he went south to Ormond Beach and the sprawling Ormond Inn, then headed to his own town of Palm Beach, and its neighbor, West Palm Beach, finally reaching the tiny trading post of Miami in 1896.

From Miami, he completed 128 miles of overwater rails to Key West in 1912. As the rails rolled, so came settlers. With Plant's young rail line in 1881, Florida had a total of 500 miles of track; by the 1890s, over 3,000 miles, with Flagler's Key West line yet to be built; and Miami was soon to experience a 1,200 percent growth in a single year.

Within the Flagler epoch, it is easy to get lost—mired in tales of the rails, the hotels, Palm Beach, Miami, the Overseas Railroad, The Breakers, even the alleged "bought legislature," the "Flagler Divorce Law," the Kenans and the resulting Binghams of Louisville, the Julia Tuttle orange blossom saga. All these stories only scratch the surface. Better to set forth a chronology of Flagler as he drove his empire the length of his new gameboard.

Flagler's "discovery" of Florida and St. Augustine in the 1880s almost parallels that of Menendez' founding of St. Augustine in 1565. Menendez opened an entirely new world, just as Flagler would open a new world for investors, pioneers, and settlers with his rails.

1883—Flagler discovers St. Augustine. Builds renaissance Ponce de Leon Hotel. Attracts America's Eastern "elite." Briefly creates "Newport of the South." Begins to drive rails south to Ormond Beach, next town.

1892—Purchases sprawling Ormond Inn, new terminus for his rails. Buys small, struggling rail lines. Creates new Florida East Coast Railway (the FEC), his new giant.

1892-93—On to Palm Beach—his own creation, and new terminus for his rails. Builds new hotels.

1894-96—Great Freeze and Julia Tuttle orange blossom bring Flagler to Miami. First train many locals have ever seen. Flagler opens Royal Palm Hotel. Miami begins to siphon off tourists from North Florida. Flagler's Ponce de Leon Hotel in St. Augustine becomes handsome girls' college. His Cordoba Hotel becomes County Courthouse, and his Alcazar is City Hall. Flagler "ghost" lives on in St. Augustine.

1899—Florida legislature becomes another part of Flagler saga—"Flagler Divorce Law" comes into being, one divorce occurs, law is rescinded.

1904—Flagler makes decision to go to Key West. Creates Overseas Railroad—the Train that Went to Sea, Eighth Wonder of the World—bringing Key Westers first train many of them have ever seen. It costs eight years of work and 700 lives.

1912—Flagler arrival in Key West sparks giant, three-day, city-wide celebration. Flagler is eighty-two.

1913—Flagler dies; $300 million fortune goes to third wife, Mary Lily Kenan Flagler, who shortly marries her prep-school lover, becomes Mary Lily Kenan Flagler Bingham, and "seeds" the Louisville Bingham media empire. But that's another story.

This rugged work site provided camping facilities, shacks, and food for hundreds of workers during construction of rails to Key West. (Courtesy Florida State Photographic Archives)

There's so much in the "Flagler File," let's just touch on a few items for those of you who are really following along.

Beginning in 1883, all his buildings were to be painted "Flagler Yellow" with bold green shutters. The Ormond Inn, the largest wooden structure in the world, had eleven miles of porches, a lobby the size of a baseball diamond, and was open—as all Flagler hotels—only for "The Season," 100 days from Christmas to Easter. It was simply called "The Ormond."

As the area became famous for auto racing, Flagler added the fabled "Ormond Garage" so car racers might tinker with their "machines." Some of the "tinkerers" would include Barney Oldfield, Ralph dePalma, William K. Vanderbilt, Ransom E. Olds, and Henry Ford. It was here the Stanley brothers brought their crazy, steam-driven car, the Stanley Steamer, to set the world's first auto-speed record.

At one point, all Flagler hotels were said to be able to house 40,000 guests at one time along Florida's east coast.

Flagler and all the railroaders were given vast lands for every mile of track laid; much of it quickly sold to speculators for $1.25 to $1.50 an acre. The "railmen" proved they were not always the "white-hat" fellows portrayed in the rail press. In some cases, homesteaded land prices grew from $150 an acre to $1,000, where Flagler rails were known to be coming.

The magic of the rails literally created towns. As rails ran from West Palm Beach to Miami, new settlements would spring up along the right-of-way. First was Linton, now Delray Beach, where the Orange Grove House of Refuge had already existed. North of Delray was the town of Lake Worth, south was Yamato, then Boca Raton, Deerfield, Dania, and Ojus. Flagler even offered one free round trip on his rails to any settler who bought land.

For all his successes, Flagler was not infallible. As his rails raced to Miami, the question of the new town of Ft. Lauderdale was brought up. Flagler was said to have commented, "This town will never be anything more than a fishing village for my guests. Let's bypass it."

When it came to waste disposal, Flagler's first plan was simply to dump all wastes into the Miami River, passing on huge problems to future generations. And in one instance, town officials in tiny Cocoanut Grove were said to have stated publicly to Flagler, "Leave us alone!"

THE CELESTIAL AND THE EIGHTH WONDER OF THE WORLD!

Flagler wanted to have his new Biltmore Hotel ready for guests in Palm Beach when his own rails were ready to bring them there. The hotel was to exceed even his own Ormond Inn—a main dining room seating 1,600 people, and vast verandahs, lobbies, and lounges. His only option was to transport building supplies via a tiny railroad running through the towns of Venus, Jupiter, Juno, and Mars, ending at the north tip of Lake Worth, where he could load supplies to his own boats. The rail was called—what else?—the Celestial Railroad. Its one engine faced only one direction, going forward on the southbound run, then backing up all the way to its starting point, since the line possessed no roundhouse, nor any means for a locomotive to turn around.

Flagler tried to buy the line in 1893. Its owners, feeling they had a good deal carrying Flagler's freight, put an exorbitant price on it. Flagler patiently waited, paying the high freight rates while quietly completing his own rails nearby. In one twelve-month period, the little rail line was said to have reaped a $68,000 harvest of Flagler dollars to transport his supplies.

The economic windfall of the tiny line was short-lived, as Flagler knew it would be. On rejection of his purchase offer, Flagler simply had his rails bypass all the towns served by the little railroad, leaving them to wither and die off to the side of the "mainstream of Florida and Flagler's rails. . . ." If the rails don't come to your town, you just don't have a town—at least not in 1892.

The Flagler epoch in Florida simply defies belief. Its final chapter was reached in 1912, when the Railroad that Went to Sea arrived in Key West. The eight-year construction project had consumed over thirty million Flagler dollars. In the project's first year, during the summer of 1905, a hurricane swept out to sea a workboat with 150 men on board.

Survivors turned up as far away as Liverpool, England, having been picked up far out in the ocean.

The work force averaged over 3,000 men at any given time. Work took four years to reach Knight's Key, halfway to Key West. Just ahead would be Bahia Honda Bridge, to be 36,000 feet in length. It would be just one more in a list of seemingly unreachable goals.

It was here the largest sea specimen ever taken was found. Near the Knightsbridge channel, a giant whale shark, said to have beached itself in shallow water, was taken up on chains and derrick. Reportedly from twenty-four to thirty thousand pounds, the behemoth was later strapped to a flatcar and displayed on tour by fishing guide Charlie Thompson.

Hurricanes continued to hamper work. Following the major blow in 1905, there were two in 1906, one in 1907, another in 1909, and one in 1910. The most severe, in 1906, blew most of the workboats out to sea. Boats broke loose, one with seventy men aboard, and simply blew away. Survivors turned up again from London to Buenos Aires.

During construction, Key West promoters sent "booze boats," in spite of no-drinking rules. Local settlements sent "preacher boats," and other opportunists sent "women boats," all serving the needs of the workers.

Completed in 1912, by 1921, it was deemed unprofitable by Flagler's FEC, and was finally sold to the state for prices reported to be between three hundred and six hundred thousand dollars, much less than it cost Flagler to build.

The ultimate storm, Labor Day 1935, almost twenty-five years after completion of the Eighth Wonder of the World, blew rolling stock, men, rails, and bridges out to sea. This small but ferocious storm, the most powerful in history, drove the barometric pressure to its lowest level in man's history—26.36 inches, 5 inches below normal. Just as from a giant saucer, the sea lifted itself from its bed and rolled over the land.

Winds were estimated at over two hundred miles per hour, and maintained this strength for up to seven hours. The estimate of two hundred mph winds was reached by engineers computing the force necessary to blow an entire train, loaded with people, off its tracks and out to sea—since all wind gauges had long since been blown away, along with the buildings to which they were attached.

This behemoth beached itself at Knight's Key, was hauled on block and tackle by Flagler's rail workers, and was displayed around the U.S. by fishing guide Charlie Thompson. (Courtesy Florida State Photographic Archives)

From the famous Hampton Dunn collection comes this shot of the Midway Inn, Snake Creek, in the Keys in the mid-1930s. Beside a blinding-white crushed-rock roadway in white sands, the inn featured clean indoor restrooms, Pure gas, a U R Welcome sign over the front door, a trailer park, rooms, cabins, and "eats." No traveller could ask for more.

Water driven by such winds smashed everything in its path, ripping steel rails, twisting them like toothpicks, and sweeping train cars out to sea. Only one locomotive remained on the track, its weight sufficient to withstand the winds. A rescue train from Miami had to "back" all the way down the Keys, arriving too late. Over five hundred highway workers were lost, and from a World War I encampment and several CCC Boys' Camps, over seven hundred more lives were unaccounted for. The storm, one of the worst disasters in U.S. history, along with the Galveston storm and Johnstown Flood, still ranked well behind Florida's 1928 blow, which took some three thousand lives.

Florida immediately began to build the Overseas Highway, using some of the old roadbed of the rails for the new auto roadway. The narrow, two-land road opened in 1938-39, lined on both sides by gleaming white gravel "fill," followed by the emerald water; always the water.

As the writer toured the new Overseas Highway in its first year of existence, the modest monument along the roadway was still brand new. It told of the 500 workers lost in the 1935 storm, just 3 1/2 years before.

However, the six hurricanes and 700 lives lost during work on the railroad, the 500 lost during the 1935 blow, and the estimated 700 more unaccounted for totalled nearly 2,000 lives from 1905 to 1935, attached to this final chapter of the Flagler Florida saga.

Today's incredible population sprawl is called, simply, "The Keys." No matter where one travels on the planet, two words—The Keys—carry a very special meaning to children of Florida.

THE GREAT FLAGLER
DIVORCE LAW MYSTERY

The great Flagler Divorce Law mystery is well chronicled by the Florida legislature (also sometimes called "The Flagler Legislature" at the time, by its detractors). The man was alleged to have literally "bought" the 1899 Florida legislature. Over four hundred documents from those involved attest to the events. No finer source could exist than legislative historian and eminent author of the *Florida Handbook,* Allen Morris.

The 1899 legislature, including the grandfather of the author, passed what became known as "The Flagler Divorce Law." Some twenty to fifty thousand 1901 dollars were said to have changed hands, the legislature passed the bill, Mr. Flagler got his divorce, the legislature rescinded the law, and only one divorce was ever granted under the unique state law — Flagler's.

Among the records of Rep. Marion S. Knight, of Lake City, no trace of voting record, gifts, or monies has ever been found. Funds and records simply disappeared into thin air. Probably some kinfolk around Florida are still looking.

Although it is difficult to trace, it was said that if a legislator could not be bought, Flagler's minions simply arranged to make a handsome gift to the man's constituency.

The chronology of the Flagler Divorce Law was made possible by Allen Morris and his vast files, Miss Lassie Goodbread Black and lawyer A. K. Black of Lake City, as well as Hampton Dunn's great collection of picture postcards in his book *Wish You Were Here.*

In 1899-1901, much state "press" did not side with the legislature at all. There was much coverage about alleged gifts, but the law was passed.

On August 21, 1901, seven days after his divorce was granted, Flagler announced his engagement to Miss Mary Lily Kenan; he was seventy-one, she was thirty-four.

To any serious history fan, the immediate question arises, "Why a Flagler divorce in Florida at all? Why Florida?" We thought you'd never ask.

Flagler, a New York resident, was apparently determined to prove his second wife, Alice Shourds, mentally unstable, have her placed in an institution, get a divorce, and marry Kenan. His lawyers found that New York state laws allowed divorce only for two reasons: desertion and adultery. Unable to pursue his project in New York, Flagler made Florida his legal residence and set about to see what the good old Cracker boys might come up with.

By 1899, the state legislature, for whatever reasons, began plans to pass the Flagler Divorce Law. Flagler was able to have his wife institutionalized in New York, get his divorce, and begin a new life with his third wife. But there is still more!

After Flagler's death in 1913, Mary Lily inherited the bulk of his vast fortune, estimated to be $300 million. Within two years, Kenan married her prep-school lover from many years prior, Robert Bingham. Mary Lily then added a codicil to her will, giving her new husband $5 million of Flagler's dollars— and within about six weeks, she died under mysterious circumstances.

The $5 million provided seed money for the entire Bingham dynasty of Louisville—newspapers, radio, TV, ambassadorship, and all.

The only way to digest it all is to get Sallie Bingham's book, *Passion and Prejudice,* and let Ms. Bingham guide you through the maze of events, even including the then-taboo subject of latent venereal disease; events that made the family into major TV talk-show material in the 1980s, and led to major courtroom battles and the eventual sale of the Bingham media dynasty.

The epoch of Flagler and his adopted Cracker gameboard covered a scant thirty years—1883 to 1913—in which the man walked, larger than life, over the land, and chose Florida as his stage. Florida would never be the same after Flagler.

THE LAND BARONS BEGIN TO ARRIVE

The empire builders, land barons, and even robber barons all became a part of the Florida to be. Some went into politics, but all simply called the shots, leaving their stamp on the state. Hordes of settlers followed the "barons," pouring into the state for about a half-century, 1890 to 1940.

Only one season showed a lull in the race toward tomorrow. Crowds of 100,000 in 1884-85 dropped to only 50,000 in 1886-87. The reason was the California Gold Rush, a portent of things to come in Florida's land boom, just ahead in the 1920s.

A review of personalities and their contributions seems never ending. There was the little-known impact of Odet Phillippe, developer of the North Tampa Bay area of Safety Harbour, but also the man who brought the grapefruit to

Florida from the Bahamas, helping create Florida as a world leader in citrus.

Carl Fisher was the Indiana boy who helped develop the auto headlight, the Indianapolis Speedway, and Miami Beach; the man about whom Will Rogers wrote, "He was first to discover land underneath all that water—land that supported the national emblem of Florida . . . the real-estate sign. . . ." Fisher came to Miami in 1910 and bought worthless swampland on Miami's Biscayne Bay islands. This provided security for a loan to John Collins for a preposterous idea—a bridge across Biscayne Bay! Fisher received island acreage for his investment, developed his lands, and rode the land boom, while his holdings soared 200 times in value in a matter of months.

Fisher's next idea was cross-country roads; one from Washington, D.C. to California, and one from Duluth to Miami. As you drive U.S. 27 down the central "spine" of Florida, you are driving Fisher's "dream highway," planned to encourage long-distance driving—which would use cars, which would need headlights so folks could drive after sundown, which would sell more headlights. The man had ideas.

His last idea was to develop Montauk Point, Long Island, into a "Miami Beach of the North." He sank his $50 million paper fortune into the project, forgetting that Montauk waters can freeze in winter.

As Nixon Smiley recounts, Fisher died, almost penniless and living alone in a small cottage on Miami Beach, in 1939. It was just a decade too soon to see his great creation explode into the giant it became in Florida's postwar years of 1945-60.

It is 1913. Miami is in the grasp of a deep depression. Flagler's rails are struggling, his hotels searching for guests. Some 10 percent of the 12,000 residents are out of work.

This was the setting in which James Deering of International Harvester discovered a tropical hammock of 160 acres on Biscayne Bay. He bought it from his neighbor, William Jennings Bryan—who had purchased an original tract from Mary Brickell for the princely sum of $25,000 seasons before. Here, Deering planted his lush, tropical-gardens estate, Villa Vizcaya, an American palace.

Creating 1,000 jobs, the palace eventually required 100 servants to maintain. Deering actually built himself a modest hideaway, across the bay on Key Biscayne. Vizcaya had cost fifteen to twenty million dollars, and had taken five years to build. Deering spent only some three hundred days in his palace during the last nine years of his life, until his death in 1925 at age sixty-six.

It's a Sunday afternoon in the land boom. In Miami, busloads of eager buyers are driven to a remote section of southwest Dade County, to a place bearing the unlikely name of Coral Gables! A young developer, George Merrick, has created a winding, Venetian pool, called "The World's Most Beautiful Swimming Pool." His busses bring crowds to his development. He also brings in, to entertain the throngs, the nation's leading orchestra, the entire Paul Whiteman Band, playing for Sunday afternoon tea dances.

And to sell the lots, standing on a platform addressing the crowds, was his top real-estate salesman, lawyer, and presidential candidate—none other than the ubiquitous William Jennings Bryan. Merrick paid Bryan $100,000 for the season: $50,000 in cash and $50,000 in lots. Merrick only went first class.

The Florida magnet never seemed to wear out. Mail-order insurance king John D. MacArthur eventually acquired some two hundred thousand acres of Florida and became one of the largest landowners in the state. By the 1950s and 1960s, MacArthur oversaw his business empire from a corner table just inside the coffee-shop entrance of his own, slightly shabby Colonnades Hotel, on the North Palm Beach island bearing the name of a baron from a previous era, Paris Singer. Singer was a backer of Addison Mizner in the 1920s.

Over several old cups of coffee, surrounded by scraps of paper and telephones, dressed in a nondescript sweatshirt and slacks, the tycoon ruled his landholdings, car rental firm, radio and TV stations, and MacArthur Scotch.

The MacArthur "touch" surfaced in the 1970s, as the landowner bought the old Biltmore Hotel in Palm Beach to save it from the wrecker's ball. Built as The Alba in the twenties, and never profitable, the building was sold to MacArthur for $5 million. Within seven years, developers converted it to condominiums, with a single unit selling for more than the original price of the entire building—the old Florida doubling game all over again.

Empire builder George Merrick's dream hotel, the centerpiece for his city of Coral Gables, was to have been his Miami Biltmore Hotel. The structure has known decades of distress, failures, closures, and various landlords and destinies since its opening in the 1920s. (Courtesy Florida State Photographic Archives)

We are indebted to Hampton Dunn for this rare, classic publicity shot of the famous Paul Whiteman Band, circa 1925. Whiteman was hired by Merrick to entertain prospects each Sunday afternoon while William Jennings Bryan sold them Coral Gables residential lots. In a stunt exactly reflective of the 1920s land boom, the band assembled in the Venetian pool for this shot. For jazz buffs, among the musicians will be found Bix Beiderbecke, Charlie Teagarden, Frankie Trumbauer, Ferdi Grofé, Mike Pingitore, and other notables. (Photo from the Hampton Dunn Collection)

Then there was Ransom E. Olds, of Oldsmobile and REO motorcar fame. Olds bought large tracts of land at the northern tip of Tampa Bay and named his town Oldsmar. Years later, citizens voted to change the name to Tampa Shores. Still later, they restored the name Oldsmar to their town.

And by the way, Henry I was honored by his Plant City, now the world strawberry capital, with the giant strawberry on top of the town water tower. It's worth a trip to see!

Near Sarasota, there was Dr. Joseph Braden, who started his "Braden Town," and built his "Braden's Castle." Its ruins still stand near the town bearing his name. And don't forget how John Ringling became totally involved with his adopted town of Sarasota, actually deeding his mansion, Ca "D" Zan, and his museums to his town.

Dr. Henry Perrine was the first man to conduct tropical-plant experiments, and to introduce the lime, lemon, and avocado to Florida. Perrine is a city just south of Miami.

The beautiful homes in Roser Park, St. Petersburg, were created by Charles Roser, bakery magnate from Ohio. Roser also went across the bay to develop lands in Bradenton. Roser is said to have given the world the Fig Newton. His fig newton allowed him to build his dream in Florida. Nowadays, some folks are saying Roser really didn't invent the fig newton after all . . . but the history books tell us he did. It's all in the history Florida isn't supposed to have any of.

And while the fig newton is pretty exciting for your average, everyday empire builder, many other inventions and discoveries played a part in Florida's expanding horizons. It was said that Tom Edison, at the time of his death, was working on a means of communicating beyond the grave. Judging from the success of Tom's other ideas, it's too bad he couldn't have stayed around. He just might have hit on something, and it could have happened in Florida, too.

Edison had two houses prefabricated in Maine and shipped to his Ft. Myers property, where they were assembled and erected—the first prefab homes. His great friend, Henry Ford, was recipient of one of the houses as a gift. In return, Ford presented Tom with that handmade flivver, its wheels widespread to match the ox-rut roads in the area.

Edison loved his wide-track flivver so much, he refused to drive anything else . . . and kept the old car for the rest of his

At this writing, the charm of the Ringling mansion, museums, and grounds in Sarasota have not diminished a single iota since their creation by the circus king. (Courtesy Florida State Photographic Archives)

One of the true visionaries, D. P. Davis dredged mud up from bay bottomlands in downtown Tampa, creating Davis Islands, here still simply white sand. One of the first structures, to left of center, is the new Davis Coliseum, sister structure to the almost identical St. Petersburg Coliseum across the bay. Few homes can be seen, and dredges are still at work in the distance, creating more land. The farthest portion would eventually become Peter O. Knight Airport. (Courtesy Florida State Photographic Archives)

life. As Ford came to realize, the gift became a pleasant alba-
tross since he was kept busy supplying handmade parts to it.
The Edison car is still on exhibit in the Edison Home and
Museum in Ft. Myers, and still is driven in the annual Edison
Festival of Light Parade, held each February in that city. (The
car also features headlights developed by Presto-Lite and Miami Beach "angel" Carl Fisher.) And the Edison Home also
features original incandescent light bulbs developed by Edison 100 years ago . . . still burning to this day!

One need not wonder as to the resources of Alred I. Du-
Pont, who moved his legal residence to Florida in 1926. Du-
Pont eventually acquired over a half-million acres of land in
the Panhandle, plus an interest in a tiny bank in Jacksonville,
the Florida National Bank. Through efforts of his principal
manager, Ed Ball, DuPont personally helped Florida through
her lean depression years, opening small DuPont banks all
over the state, giving support to local small businesses.

In 1931, the DuPont interests, through their International
Paper Co., opened a vast pulp mill near Panama City in West
Florida, with thousands of forest acres acquired. DuPont
then helped create, in 1935, the Florida Forestry Service. His
paper interests grew to become the St. Joe Paper Company,
helping the "rebirth" of tiny St. Joseph, Florida, into today's
Port St. Joe.

The interests continued to grow with the acquisition of
80,000 acres in the Wakulla area, the DuPont Forest, and
Wakulla Inn around famed Wakulla Springs, deepest in the
world.

Among the rail barons and flamboyant empire builders,
occasionally we find a down-to-earth businessman who simply saw opportunity. Such was the case with George Sebring,
who brought his family from Sebring, Ohio, a town also
founded by his clan, and settled their new town of Sebring,
Florida, to be based on the Greek city of Heliopolis, with
streets emanating from a central circle.

At the opposite end of the spectrum would be D. P. Davis,
product of tiny Green Cove Springs. Davis was to create Davis
Islands by dredging bay bottomland at Tampa, creating land
where there was none. He became an overnight success and
immediately left for St. Augustine, where he planned to du-
plicate his feat. The land boom was not to allow it. In the

bust, Davis lost his entire fortune, and lost his life, by either jumping or falling overboard.

THE MAN WHO LOVED ACRONYMS, AND OTHER INTERESTING FOLKS

The man who loved acronyms created his first one with Alcoa—Aluminum Company of America. He came to Florida, with his fortune, at age eighty-one! When most persons are content to rest on their laurels, he began an entirely new career on the gigantic Florida gameboard. He created plans requiring fifteen years to complete, when he was ninety-one!

A. V. Davis embarked on a buying spree, unmatched by any of the previous "barons," investing up to a million dollars a week in land, businesses, companies, forests . . . anything that caught his eye, it seemed, becoming Florida's largest land-holder (some 140,000 acres). As Nixon Smiley tells, at one point, Davis set his sights on the only super treasure he didn't own, the Boca Raton Hotel, then owned by Mr. Schine of the Schine Hotel Chain.

Following months of discussion, Mr. Schine apparently said, "Mr. Davis, the hotel is simply not for sale at any price."

Davis said quietly, "I'll give you $22 million" (or words to that effect).

Schine is said to have replied, "Write that down on this napkin and you've got yourself a deal."

It was apparently a case of the old "immovable-object-irresistible-force" syndrome, with shades of Irlo Bronson. Schine had recently bought the hotel complex for $1.6 million.

Now, Davis formed his second great acronym, this one bearing the first two letters of his full name: Arthur Vining Davis. He placed all his lands in the holding company, took it public, and watched the stock soar as the public gobbled up shares. Davis, over a scant thirteen years, had created Arvida, almost as an afterthought in his life.

We give special thanks to the late Cracker storyteller Nixon Smiley, for relating his unique Davis experiences.

As different from one another as the blazing sunrises of Florida's east coast are from the golden sunsets on the Gulf . . . are the personalities of Florida's empire builders.

Barron Collier, land baron who developed thousands of acres in Southwest Florida, was as low profile as Flagler was "hot copy" on the east coast. Collier's fortune, from streetcars and advertising car-cards in Baltimore and Washington, D.C., helped create a one-man land boom in the quiet southwestern corner of the gameboard. It became Collier County, but it all happened so quietly that few outsiders had accurate knowledge of its growth and dimensions.

At one time also the state's largest single landholder, Collier spearheaded the Tamiami Trail road, connecting his lands to Miami, when most felt it was doomed to failure. Collier's own brother became his "man in Tallahassee" in the legislature. Bonds to complete the road were financed by Collier banks, sold by Collier companies, promoted by Collier media, and Collier companies helped build the road, thirteen years in the making. The road would travel over incredibly forbidding terrain—the Everglades—and in the making, would cost hundreds of lives. Construction sites would be "policed" by Collier's own "Mounties," his private mounted police.

The sites would be travelled by Collier's own Trail Bus Tour Company busses, carrying fascinated tourists across the remote land to watch workers at their seemingly impossible task, and to see Collier-developed "Indian Villages" along the roadway.

The roadway, unintentionally, also became the very first man-made barrier to the one-mile-per-day natural southerly flow of Florida's vast wetlands; the first change in the eons-old water system, which would bring problems to Florida for a century to come, remaining the only such barrier until completion of the famed Alligator Alley, connecting Naples and Ft. Lauderdale, generations later.

Collier was to Southwest Florida what Flagler was to the East Coast, what Plant was to the Tampa Bay area, and what Chipley was to West Florida.

Even his tour busses bore the unmistakable Collier golden touch. They eventually grew to become National Trailways Bus System.

The name "Barron," his given name, was most apt for this empire builder of Florida. He was a man named for his destiny.

While the Panhandle remained less high profile than the state's other arenas, still, action continued throughout the area. This was Chipley Country. William D. Chipley chose to run his rails west, finding a market untapped by the other rail barons and finding fertile lands for the developing.

Chipley obtained a state grant, giving his companies 2 million acres of land, if he would build his railroad from Jacksonville west to Pensacola. Had he secured all the grants he was applying for, his rails would have owned a major part of the entire Panhandle at one time. The town bearing his name served as one of his company headquarters as his rails were being built.

With Chipley, Plant, and Flagler, S. Davies Warfield was the fourth member of the "rails quartet." The Baltimore investor drove his rails across the midsection of Florida, from the Tampa Bay area, to join with Flagler's FEC rails as they raced down the Eastern seaboard. Warfield chose wisely, since Chipley had already staked out the Panhandle, Flagler the East Coast, and Plant the Tampa Bay region.

These four men must have enjoyed incredible power. In almost every instance, if the rails didn't come to your town, you simply didn't have a town; prosperity and growth followed the rails. Henry Plant's decision to bypass the tiny town of Cedar Key and drive his rails instead to Tampa made the latter city's population soar. Flagler's bypass of the tiny Celestial Rail towns of Juno, Jupiter, Venus, and Mars postponed growth of the first two of these towns for a century, and assured the demise of the other two. The well-established resort town and hotel at Flamingo, Florida, simply faded from existence when the rails bypassed the town. And Hamilton Disston's dream for Disston City crashed as each rail was turned toward Tampa Bay and downtown St. Petersburg, literally reversing his plan for his town of Disston City—later Gulfport.

THE IRON HORSE COMES TO ST. PETE

It's 1939—a chilly, Sunday afternoon—and S. Davies Warfield is about to have an indelible effect on the lives of hundreds of Florida depression kids, along with a brand new thing called a streamlined train!

Warfield placed dining-car service on the rails from New York to Miami. A sleek, bullet-shaped locomotive pulled aluminum-sheathed cars, which gleamed in the sun, appearing silver as they streaked through the countryside.

In its initial run, the gleaming train paid a visit to St. Petersburg along its way. Families climbed through weed-choked creek-beds, backroads, alleys, and lined the trash-strewn tracks of the Seaboard. Kids held their breath, put their ears down on the tracks to see if they could hear a hum of wheels on rail, and listened for the strange, new sound of a diesel horn they'd heard about, instead of the old, familiar train whistle.

The monolith came slowly down the tracks on that cold Sunday afternoon. Families lined the tracks, holding small kids back from the rails, but as close as they dared to the behemoth . . . as the gleaming train made its way through the neighborhoods, where both sides of the tracks were the wrong side of the tracks. Families stood in awe as the huge machine came rumbling—no, gliding is a better word—with giant engines humming. The cars seemed to stretch on for miles.

Children stared transfixed, in the weed-choked ditches, getting as close as we dared to watch the giant train pass, heading for the old Seaboard station downtown. We could not have known we were looking at the world's largest and most powerful locomotive ever built—courtesy of Mr. S. Davies Warfield.

As the reader may imagine, it was a memorable day for thousands of Florida depression kids, including the author— the day the Silver Meteor came to town. From the diesel horn alone, the romance of the rails would never be the same.

THINGS ARE GETTING SERIOUS; MR. GEIST COMES TO TOWN

Empire builders came in all shapes and sizes. One was even nicknamed "Water Boy."

Clarence H. Geist had made his fortune investing in water companies, having migrated from an Indiana farm to Pennsylvania, then, with fortune in hand, to Florida's Palm

In February 1939 in Jacksonville, the massive Silver Meteor began its very first run south, making a special stop in St. Petersburg. The famous Union Terminal Station can be seen in the background mists of this Jacksonville picture. (Courtesy Florida State Photographic Archives)

This classic photo from Peg McCall and Sue McDermitt of the Boca Raton Historical Society, and from the Historical Society of South Florida, combines several vital factors. CENTER: The fledgling Boca Raton Hotel, The Cloisters, beside raw undeveloped land. UPPER CENTER: Its golf course, just graded and showing only gleaming white sands. LOWER CENTER: The path of the new channel, which will become the Intracoastal Waterway, as it cuts through what will become Lake Boca. The gleaming white swatch curving from the upper left corner to the right center will become the 130-foot-wide Camino Real Boulevard. Mizner envisioned a canal down its center, with guests arriving by Venetian gondola. The marshy islands would eventually be filled to become the ocean beach and the other shore of Lake Boca. This single picture captures the evolution of the entire area in a sweeping view.

Beaches. He was said by some to be arrogant and pompous, with an incredible inferiority complex, and was snubbed by Palm Beach society. Geist then decided to have his *own* club, and cast an eye on the bankrupt Boca Raton Hotel, dream of the Mizners a couple seasons before.

It was 1928. Florida was in the process of experiencing two killer hurricanes, plus her own incredible land boom and bust—her very own depression—and unaware that the stock-market crash and national depression lurked just over the horizon.

The Mizner dream world had collapsed and Geist simply picked up the pieces. He bailed out the hotel company, and created in Boca Raton one of the most incredible fiefdoms ever to exist in Florida.

As friend Nixon Smiley said, "Stories about Geist have to be fiction. . . . They're too wild to be fact" (including the story of Geist being snubbed by the Everglades Club, since Smiley said no one would have ever put his name up anyway). But back to Mr. Geist.

Let us list some items and trivia—some apocryphal and others well documented, including Smiley's rare, firsthand interview items shared with us by Nixon from his personal notes. Sometimes, truth is stranger than fiction.

In the trivia department, stories of guests decorating their own hotel suites, plus cottages for their servants, pale alongside the real Geist stories. We'll start with the easy ones first. Hang on; here we go.

A) No one was allowed to register in the hotel unless approved by Geist.

B) Geist would tap a guest on the shoulder with his cane and shout, "I own this hotel. Who are you?"

C) After golf, he might change clothes, passing through the lobby in his bathrobe.

D) If playing golf, he was often followed around the course by his chauffeur-driven limousine, actually driven down the fairways and around the greens—the world's largest golf cart.

E) Boarding an elevator filled with guests, Geist would shout, "Six." The attendant would take him to his suite, then meekly drop off the other guests at their requested floors. It was unique customer relations, Geist style.

F) Evening movies at the hotel would start only at Geist's arrival; he would stomp to the front row, gaze over the guests, and shout, "I'm here!"

G) He would often leave during the film, ending the showing. The film would simply be stopped, and guests would drift out of the theater.

H) If he didn't like a $420,000 carpet, he would simply spit on it.

I) He overlorded the tiny town of Boca Raton—with its 600 people—poking any nearby citizen with his cane, demanding, "Do you know who I am?" Since most depended on Geist for a living, yes, they did.

J) He ran the town politically as well. He had the town charter rewritten to have elections in February instead of November, so his staff could vote, whether town residents or not, whether they could read and write or not, or even speak English.

K) A virtual comic-opera scene was acted out at beginning and end of each winter season. All employees of the hotel were summoned to a command performance to greet Geist as he arrived in his private rail car at the tiny Boca Raton terminal. The hotel orchestra would "play him off the train," and escort him to his castle. In spring, a reversal of the Gilbert and Sullivan tableau would take place, as he left for his Northern residence. Even Flagler, Plant, and probably William the Conquerer never pulled this one off.

L) In one story, Geist is said to have been "topped" in only one instance; he snarled at a caddy as the boy lit a cigarette. The caddy snarled back, shouting, "You can't order me around like you do everyone else, you S.O.B. I'll tell you just what people think of you," which he did, threw down the golf bag, and walked away.

In the best Horatio Alger tradition, Geist is said to have barked, "Bring that kid here. I want him back." The caddy simply refused, adding another charming "Florida first" on that fateful day in old Boca Raton.

But wait, There's more.

M) Geist lived in mortal fear of his own death. He kept two

burly guards on twenty-four-hour watch, and a killer police dog in his sitting room.

N) He moved among several suites, finally building a private elevator—its key under special guard so his presence would never be known.

O) Hotel entrance gatekeepers always kept shotguns and pistols at the ready, within easy reach.

P) And finally, he kept one of the largest checking accounts in the world at the time, with $1 million in ready cash, just in case of ransom needs.

It must be concluded that he gave a new meaning to the words "baron," "empire builder," and probably "paranoia." As his cronies said, "The ransom money was silly. No one who ever knew him would ever want to kidnap him."

His name is also commemorated in the beautiful Geist Reservoir, northeast of Indianapolis, a long-ago part of the Geist Water Company interests and an example of the potential of Florida's water system in the century ahead; to include lakes, ponds, and reservoirs, dotting the landscape, all interconnected by a scenic water-delivering canal system.

The incredible Clarence H. Geist was a truly unique Indiana export to Florida.

THE GRANDEST VISIONARY OF THEM ALL

So little has been written about Hamilton Disston, although he was an empire builder who had one of the greatest effects on Florida and did it all a quarter-century before most of the "builders" began to discover the Magic Land gameboard.

It is just after the Civil War. Florida's controversial land sale has set aside millions of acres of land to be sold at auction, along with gifts of millions more to rail barons. Given these policies, the state treasury is only a few steps away from bankruptcy. With Florida finances a shambles, Governor John Milton, for whom the town of Milton had been named, takes his own life, stating he prefers death to Reconstruction. Such was the economic condition of Florida in 1868.

At the same time, the federal government was giving 165-acre parcels of land to any settler who would live on the land, farm it, and improve it. Settlers in Florida found it took 20 acres just to feed a mule. Many simply left. They could not survive on the land.

All this led to the state "land plan" wherein Florida would sell land to settlers, for about $1.25 an acre. With various interests taking all sides, the plan grew in controversy.

By 1881, Florida's land policies were in disarray, her finances a disaster, her leadership fragmented (including the suicide of the governor), and her land-sale plan under fire from all sides.

In 1880, Florida's new governor, William Bloxham, had been elected partly through his promise to—of all things—drain the Everglades, making land attractive to settlers.

Florida was also struggling into the rail era, with fewer than five hundred miles of track in the state, and only two miles completed in fourteen years—from 1866 to 1880.

With massive land giveaways to railmen in the land-sale plan, farmers still suffered from choking rail rates, though in many cases the farmers were the very ones who "mortgaged the farm" to help bring the rails to their town.

Into this scenario, with his Disston Saw Company family fortune, comes Hamilton Disston and his associates. He brought a satchel full of greenbacks—one million of them (figuratively speaking, of course). We may only envision a scene taken from every Western movie ever produced, where Mr. Disston comes into the land office, plunks down a satchel on the counter, and faces the land clerk.

CLERK: "What's in the satchel, mister?"

DISSTON: "I got here $1 million, cash-money, boys." (Folks from Philadelphia probably didn't talk thataway, but no matter.)

CLERK: "What you want for it?"

DISSTON: "I'll take 1 million acres of that land you got on sale. Give you twenty-five cents an acre for it." (He sounds like a friend of Irlo Bronson.)

CLERK: "Well, we'd better have a meeting on this." (Land board retires to back room, chuckling.)

(Land board returns to counter, still chuckling.)

CLERK: "Well sir, only land we can let you have at that price is some old swamp, down south." (In those days, they called things by their right names. Swamp was swamp.)

DISSTON: "OK boys, I'll take it."

CLERK: "What you gonna do with all that swamp, mister?"

DISSTON: "Boys, I'm gonna drain that sucker."

CLERK: "Well, in that case, reckon we better have another meeting."

(Land board retires to back room, then returns, still chuckling. Got a live one . . .)

CLERK: Tell you what we're goin' to do. We got 2 million more acres of swamp we're goin' to let you drain, and we'll give you half of whatever you drain. How's that for a deal?"

End of scene. Curtain.

In that instant, Disston controlled 6 million acres of Florida—virtually the entire lower-central section, from near Orlando to south of Lake Okeechobee, the largest single land-acquisition transaction by one man in the history of the continent.

Controversy erupted from many quarters. Florida's bonds were creeping toward default. Some said the land price was so low that the rights of land-squatters were being violated. In fact, Disston did have a contract to drain land, in return for half of all lands he could drain, but the courts would not approve such a plan, so Governor Bloxham persuaded Disston to first buy some land to cement the deal.

Disston, however, was allowed to choose much that wasn't swampland within his 4-million-acre purchase. As well, squatters were given two more years to complete their own purchase of lands.

Included in Disston's land was some one hundred fifty thousand acres along the lower edge of Pinellas County, fronting on today's Boca Ciega Bay, where he built his own town, Disston City. It was planned to be his crowning achievement, as he was led to believe an agreement existed whereby the oncoming Seaboard rails would terminate at his bayfront property, helping create a major, dynamic city.

All history includes countless tiny quirks that bring about vast changes for generations to come. In just such a move, S. Davies Warfield, for reasons best known to himself, turned his rails eastward to the equally tiny town of St. Petersburg, to end his rails on the Tampa Bay side of the peninsula, ignoring the Boca Ciega Bay shore owned by Disston. Disston was to learn the axiom proven time and again by Florida's rail barons. If the rails don't stop at your town, you don't have a town.

In that single move, the destiny of the two towns was forged. St. Pete was to enjoy the next hundred years of growth with shops, waterfront yachts, and the famed Million Dollar Pier, while Disston City was moved to a "shadow role," Disston interests being bailed out by creditors. Changing its name to Gulfport, today it is a fascinating time-warp of a town, locked in 1934.

One of few reminders of this special dream was in Disston Junior High School, on Disston Avenue, from which many distinguished personages have graduated (or at least attended briefly).

Disston's main dream continued as he eventually drained about one-sixth of his lands, with the present towns of Kissimmee and St. Cloud, including the world's most famous tourist destination, all resting partially on lands created by Hamilton Disston. You just gotta love the guy.

Downtown Gulfport remains a walk through yesteryear, with narrow, uneven brick streets lined by ancient, tiny buildings; the original Gulfport Casino; the old once-proud Gulfport Inn, still standing, though boarded up; and little houses, block after block with not a single change for fifty years as if awaiting the magic hand of another Hamilton Disston to wave the wand of development money and create instant new horizons. Indeed, it may happen in this antique town someday.

In the economic downturn of 1894-95, accompanying the Great Freeze, Disston's fortune sadly eroded. The visionary took his own life at fifty-two years of age. His family lost interest in developing his city, and the Disston chapter of Florida's history came to an undeserved end. Disston, planning his dream city, simply guessed wrong as the rails bypassed one town in favor of another.

CHAPTER 6

The Land Boom

IF THEY'RE SELLING YOU PIE IN THE SKY, THEY'RE GONNA MAKE IT WITH YOUR DOUGH

Imagine a sales campaign for a very special product—a product so special that millions of people would try to get in on the deal. Now add to this the fact that one-half the entire population of the nation would have to move their residences to justify the sales effort of the product. Add these factors together and you have a thumbnail sketch of the grandest land adventure in all America's history, with the fastest fast-buck artists, the smoothest-talking con men, the sharpest land sharks, and the biggest dollars in the land. All came together in one arena: Florida.

Hang on. It's the Florida land boom!

Florida in the 1920s was hustlers, real-estate salesmen and -women, the Binder Boys, promoters, and wheeler-dealers. They were all a part of Florida's golden decade.

The boom started with the empire builders, following the Civil War, building a head of steam by the 1880s with visionaries such as Disston-saw heir Hamilton Disston, with his dream of draining the Everglades to create *more* land from which he might make an even grander fortune. By the 1890s, Florida towns were springing up like wild flowers. Land

173

barons came, buying huge tracts of raw land, platting entire towns, bringing settlers to fill their lands, and building their roads and rails. It became "Florida fever," all leading to the Golden Decade, 1919-28.

During the boom, many cities were born. In Miami alone, the towns of Coral Gables, Opa-Locka, and Hialeah were born within months of one another as the boom roared by. The Miami *Daily News*, in 1925, published the largest newspaper ever printed; the single issue of 504 pages weighed 7 1/2 pounds.

The boom's "surge" began with a national restlessness following World War I, with millions of people moving about the country, seeking a new life. Some returned to wartime haunts, including Florida, which they had discovered during a military assignment. The migration targeted certain areas: central Florida/Orlando, the Tampa Bay region, the far west around Pensacola, northeast Florida/Jacksonville, and the lower southeast coast/Palm Beach-Miami. While all Florida would experience some of the effects of the boom, these five "new frontiers," especially Tampa Bay and the southeast coast, would be its pulsating heart.

Thousands came, buying land, often with only paper to support the transaction. They created countless "boomlets," supporting countless promoters, new developments, and dream cities. The dreams were often bordered by handsome gates, leading nowhere. Behind the gates were hundreds of thousands of acres, awaiting a magic wand that was to create sparkling cities of gold!

While the "Roaring Twenties" were roaring all over the nation, in the North the excitement was centered around "paper millionaires," the stock market, new industries, and new factories. In Florida, it was an entirely different story. Florida had only one asset going for her . . . and on sale—land!

She was about to go land mad. Within a single decade, Florida's entire economy was caught up in a feeling of eternal prosperity with promoters on every corner ready to prove the euphoria was genuine, and permanent.

The boom continued to roll through the mid-1920s, stumbling only when confronted by a major hurricane in 1926. After the storm, it crawled back to its feet, only to be dealt a deathblow by the mega-killer hurricane of 1928! Gasping for

Just prior to the land boom years, Ft. Myers promoted its new yacht club (circa 1913) with techniques that were years ahead of their time. (Courtesy Florida State Photographic Archives)

Tampa's population would soar to 90,000 by the late 1940s, double by the 1950s, double again by the 1960s, and double again by the 1980s. To the upper right of center is Plant's fabled Tampa Bay Hotel/University of Tampa. At the far left is the bridge to Davis Islands, and the radio tower downtown is WDAE, Florida's first licensed radio station. (Courtesy Florida State Photographic Archives)

breath, it still crept to its knees. Looking up, it stared straight ahead, straight into the face of Black Tuesday, October 29, 1929. Florida had been dealt not one, not two, but three major blows within thirty-six months, blows striking directly at a momentum that had been surging across the land since the 1880s.

The Florida land boom was to equal all the gold rushes on the continent put together. It generated entire cities, towns, companies, railroads, scams, scandals, and scoundrels, each staking out his personal "turf." In Miami, it meant Carl Fisher with his dream city Miami Beach and George Merrick with his Coral Gables. Merrick was to become a one-man land boom.

Up the coast, it meant Joseph Young and his "Hollywood-by-the-Sea," created from acres of wasteland. In the Palm Beaches, it meant Singer Sewing Machine heir Paris Singer and the "Eccentric Mizners," with their "I am the world's greatest resort" ads for their new town called "Boca Raton." Singer also helped promoter Harry Kelsey with his "Kelsey City" dream.

In the far southwest, it meant the all-pervading name of Barron Collier. Up the Gulf Coast, it meant the "Fearsome Foursome of Ft. Myers."

In Tampa, it meant flamboyant D. P. Davis and his Davis Islands. Across the bay, in St. Petersburg, it meant many promoters: Walter Fuller, Perry Snell with his posh Snell Isle homes, and A. C. Pheil and Charles Roser, who brought his "fig-newton fortune" from Ohio to become a "boomer." And, of course, it meant "Handsome Jack" Taylor and his bout with the famed "Backwards-Spelling Tooth Fairy," resulting in his Rolyat Hotel!

In the northeast, in Green Cove Springs, it meant the on-going work of J. C. Penney, Gail Borden, the Hoover vacuum-cleaner interests, Mr. Lynch of Merrill Lynch, and Grover Cleveland, continuing their momentum from forty years before. The barons were creating new cities where the pioneers had created settlements and villages.

In addition to the "mighty," the boom meant hordes of ordinary, "little people" pouring into Florida, seeking to tap into the "get-rich-quick" magic they'd heard so much about. The great and the small travelled together along the upside

While the boom's pulsating hearts were the southeast coast and Tampa Bay regions, the "Florida fever" caught on all over. This was early land-auction action in Escambia County in the Panhandle at a planned townsite, circa 1920. The tents would be set up at the main cross streets of the town-to-be. (Courtesy Florida State Photographic Archives)

This standard ad from the mid-1920s was in the Panhandle near the town of Monticello, showing a street grid of "Monticello Suburbs." These grids would dot the Florida landscape for generations to come. (Courtesy Florida State Photographic Archives)

of the mountain, scarcely thinking there might be a downside as well, just ahead. It was the boom. And Florida was golden forever!

IT'S LAND, LAND, LAND, AND THEY AIN'T MAKIN' ANYMORE

The power and momentum of the boom was so great that even Florida's population reflected its surges. West Palm Beach, a major player on the gameboard, soared to 30,000 people by 1930—four times its population of about a decade earlier. Most cities in the path of the boom grew until 1929-30, when the growth suddenly stopped, as if a giant curtain had come down on a ten-year drama. Following the stock-market crash and depression, population numbers remained static until 1940 and World War II.

With an estimated population of 1 million in 1900, the estimate was only 1.2 million in 1940, forty years later; so great was the effect of the land boom and bust.

From 1920 on, however, the surge of people became so great—with action moving so fast—that areas were teeming with people, cash in hand, demanding to buy land as they sought to get in on the high-rolling action. Sellers no longer bothered showing actual property. Buyers didn't care. They just wanted the land for quick resale and profit, as fast as possible.

One tract, near Deerfield Beach in southeast Florida, sold for $50 an acre. Two days later it resold for $200 an acre. Seven days later, it drew $600 an acre; and six months later, it turned over for $5,000 an acre. Nearby, a Pompano Beach forty-acre piece that had sold for $36,000 in 1924 sold in mid-1925, twelve months later, for $1 million! Nothing on the land had changed, only the momentum of the boom.

It's the early 1920s. The pace quickens; the flow of investors increases. Dollars accumulate and prices soar. In St. Petersburg alone, within a span of just five years, no fewer than five major resort hotels came into being, plus seven smaller inns. The first was the "million-dollar hotel," The Soreno, followed by the Vinoy Park, structured as a European castle, overlooking St. Pete's also brand new Million Dollar Pier,

Charles Roser and his "fig-newton fortune" produced beautiful Roser Park in St. Pete, plus developments across the bay in Bradenton.

which would become the city's trademark for the next generation.

Shortly afterwards, only blocks away, came the Suwannee Hotel, then the Mason (later called The Princess Martha), followed by the pink palace, The Don Ce Sar on the Gulf in Pass-a-Grille. The "Don" was to experience difficulties, as did every major hotel in boomtime Florida. It was to operate as a hotel, an office building, an army hospital, an air force R&R station in World War II, and finally was restored to its original beauty as the original Don.

Then there was the Rolyat Hotel, later becoming the Florida Military Academy and still later, the Stetson University School of Law; and also the luxurious Jungle Hotel, which became the Admiral Farragut Naval Academy.

Similar track records were being set across the bay in Tampa, Winter Park, Lake Worth, Delray Beach, Boca Raton, Hollywood, Miami, and all along the Gulf from Naples to New Port Richey. And this was just in southern Florida. Similar scenes were being played to varying degrees all over the state.

The boom continues to roll. Deals turn over the same piece of land up to eight times in a single day. Much of the state is caught up in the magic.

As speculation forces prices upwards, the city of Ft. Myers annexes itself to eight times its size of ten years before. It persuades voters to approve a $3.5 million bond issue for sprawling sewer systems, roads, lights, and gas mains, reaching far into the countryside of scrub-palmetto land and little else. Ft. Myers, along with dozens of towns, staggers into financial chaos, unable to support its own bonds and boomtime debt. One hundred towns were to experience similar problems.

It's still the first half of the 1920s, and the boom is suffering from negative press attacks in Northern newspapers. One Gulf Coast newspaper, attempting to retaliate, shrieked in front-page banner headlines aimed at Northern papers, "Shut Your Damn Mouth!" Florida articles appeared that actually denied there was any "boom" at all, but simply what was termed as "healthy increases in property values . . . leading to even greater heights." As the real-estate salesman must have said to his prospect, "If you'll buy that, friend, I've got some land in the Everglades I wanna talk to you about."

The Pass-a-Grille Casino sat on the massive beach in front of the old Pass-a-Grille Inn, and today's Hurricane Restaurant, although present-day visitors find it hard to believe that there were another 100 yards of beach behind the casino. (Courtesy St. Petersburg Historical Society)

Old "Handsome Jack" Taylor's dream hotel, The Rolyat, over in Pasadena-on-the-Gulf. (Courtesy Florida State Photographic Archives)

The pace continues to quicken. It's 1923-24 and prices are soaring. Land prices in West Palm Beach are doubling within weeks. One parcel increases $750 an hour. A buyer pays $11,000 for a lot at 3:00 and sells it at 4:45 for $12,500.

In the Palm Beaches, a thirty-two-acre tract, bought from a homesteader a few seasons before for $75,000, sells in 1925 for $1 million. Within nine months, the same tract, cut into lots, brings $2 million at public auction. It's the old Florida doubling game all over again.

Into this cauldron comes a brand-new player: the Binder Boys!

THE BINDER BOYS AND THEIR ELECTRIC SALES MACHINE

The Binder Boys came to town, young men on bicycles wearing knickers (called acreage-trousers) and blazers. These standard uniforms were said to be worn so the boys might recognize each other and avoid trying to sell the same land over and over again—to each other. Binder Boys were true Florida originals. They helped fuel the wildest binge in the history of America's land-ownership.

The premise was simple. Binder Boys—supersalesmen who would stop at nothing to make a sale—would "bind" a piece of land with a token deposit, receiving a slip of paper that said, in effect, that they owned the land, although little cash had changed hands, e.g., perhaps $500 to bind a $50,000 piece with an actual down payment, say $20,000, postponed as long as possible. With no intention of ever meeting that payment, the boys would resell the binder, making a profit in the markup of the slip of paper, as they would hand it off to another speculator; each buyer assuming the price would continue to rise.

The binder might change hands many times before the last buyer would be caught with the major payment due, or with no other buyers around, or at the end of the boom. Nawww, that could never happen!

Binder Boys have been called the "growth engine" of the boom. The key was *speed*—a quick turnover, a quick profit, and on to the next deal. Instant riches.

A Palm Beach tract, sold in 1923 for $800,000, was sold again twenty-four months later for $4 million. That's respectable appreciation. A 250-lot piece in Kelsey City, estimated at about $300 per lot in 1923, went for $1.7 million in 1925. Things were going pretty good for just a bunch of good ol' boys doing a little swapping.

Part of the system also involved the time required to process and record transfer of deed, title, and land, plus delaying closing as long as possible to allow for a maximum number of binder turnovers before payment came due.

It was real-estate musical chairs and the old spoon dance all rolled into one. Gathering steam, roaring full speed ahead in 1923, the Binder Boys would be history within thirty-six months.

Indianapolis realtor Robert Walker told of how he left home as a nineteen-year-old to head for Florida to become a Binder Boy, just at the end of the boom. He went first to St. Petersburg, and then on to Miami, the big leagues.

Stuart McIver, the great chronicler of "things Broward," tells the story of N. B. T. Roney, developer of the famed Roney Plaza Hotel, becoming incensed at Binder Boys' activities, and setting up an ambush for them at his Seminole Beach project near Hallandale.

Roney was said to have sold strips of land to the boys at option prices, and then sold adjacent strips to others at sharply lowered prices, leaving the boys with no way of selling their land at a profit, forcing them to pay the piper. With no prospects to turn to, the boys, low on cash, were simply wiped out. As McIver says, it makes a great tale—e.g., "Shootout at Seminole Beach," or "Cutting the Boys Off at the Inlet"—but the truth is, sale of the Seminole land moved far too quickly to have any effect on the boys. In fact, the entire development was sold out in one incredible day!

With just a few phone calls, Roney's office was swamped with buyers. Every lot was sold, with over seven million dollars in sales before the day was over. But wait. There's more.

Within a week, all buyers were said to have resold their lots to others for over twelve million dollars . . . and within about thirty days, the great boom was imperceptibly slowing. Now the subsequent buyers found no new buyers, and had to come up with that famous second payment themselves. Many simply lost their investments, with the lots now reverting back to the original owner from whom Roney had first bought the land, a Mr. Wade Harley. With the gentle slowing of the boom, Harley had been able to "eat his cake, sell his cake, and still keep his cake," all at the same time. It was to be one of the last, fast rides on the Florida land boom merry-go-round.

THE BOOM BUILDS

By the time the boom had reached its apex—winter 1924-25—the crush of people pouring into South Florida had seen Miami explode in population; in one season, the city was said to have grown by some 1,200 percent. Population surges affected all Florida, with some areas growing at two to five times the national rate. But Southeast Florida appeared to outdistance the state and the U.S. combined.

Northern media began running editorials cautioning their citizens against "gambling on faraway lands you've never even seen." Savings and loan associations experienced such withdrawal rates that they warned depositors against using funds to gamble in Florida land. It was a tiny taste of the old robber baron action, prompting the old Cracker saying, "Remember, man will not *eat* his own kind. He will, however, skin 'em."

It's 1921. Joseph Young, a land-baron-to-be, plans his own dream town, Hollywood-by-the-Sea: streets 130 feet wide, twelve cars abreast! Giant traffic circles in the roadway would create traffic tie-ups in the 1960s and be restored in the 1990s. Young added a vast beach boardwalk, and his Hollywood Beach Hotel. The hotel, as with many of its sister structures, housed many businesses in succession—an eating establishment, an office complex, a local radio station, retail shops, and finally, after being vacant, converted back to a residential complex.

It's winter 1924-25. The boom continues to spiral upwards, the graph curve swinging straight up. More and more people pour into Ft. Myers, Tampa, St. Pete, Orlando, and West Palm Beach. In a growing competition for customers, a few flamboyant projects are quietly weakening the sound ones.

As Tarzan said to Jane, "It's a jungle out there." Property values in 1925-26 grow 560 percent in one year. Paved street permits soar from $4,000 in 1921 to $59 million just five years later.

The boom becomes the living expression of "Coolidge Prosperity." Every American deserves to be rich! Every family should have cars, homes, and the good life, and the Florida land boom—by golly—is going to provide it all!

Developer after developer comes. "Dad" Gandy, from Philadelphia, comes to St. Pete and completes his "Gandy's Folly," his crazy idea of a bridge across Tampa Bay linking the two bay cities. This creates its own "boomlet" in property values along approaches to the bridge.

Tampa's D. P. Davis sells 300 of his Davis Island lots in three hours for $1.5 million . . . lots that are still underwater. By the end of 1925, he sells out the entire development for $18 million, and goes to St. Augustine to do it over again, developing Davis Shores in that city.

Many Florida depression kids know stories of the land boom. Ill-fated Lakewood Estates in St. Petersburg deserves special mention. Most Florida developments would include a country club with the compulsory golf course, and in the case of Lakewood Estates, winding, pink concrete streets seeming to go on forever, punctuated only by driveway cuts, fire hydrants, and decorative, rococo streetlights—at least light *poles*; the large bulbs victims of long-ago BB guns. And there would be nothing else—no homes, no foundations, no construction—just streets and mysterious pine forests, stretching (to young minds) for miles and miles.

At some point in the boom, investors would simply walk away from their investment, leaving it to the banks. The banks, having little choice but to repossess the project, would "sit" on the land until a buyer could be found. From the end of the boom until the early 1950s, parts of Lakewood Estates land lay fallow in enchanted pine forests, until new investors resumed the dream that had died with the boom.

In this instance, however, a tiny benefit derived from the crash. An entire generation of Florida depression kids knew the woods only as a fantastic place for roller-skating—rolling forever on the smooth, poured-pink-concrete streets winding through the deep shade of the miles of piney woods. Perhaps only a few members of that generation will recall the magic mysteries of the strangely winding pink streets, the twisting

cracks filled with weeds, and the driveway cuts leading to absolutely nothing but deserted pine forests.

You Lakewood Estaters, under your smooth, current-day
blacktop roads, may find the original 1920s poured concrete
still faintly glowing pale pink; and if you kneel on the pavement, you may still find skid-marks of hundreds of old, strap-
on, metal-wheel roller skates.

And probably, off to the side of Serpentine Way, you may
find a long-lost skate key, which very nearly destroyed a beautiful and feverish fourth-grade relationship. If you do, would
you please mail it to the author in care of the publisher's address. We would be most appreciative.

BY THE TIME YOU CAN MAKE ENDS MEET, SOMEBODY MOVES THE ENDS

It is "season" — 1924-25. The boom continues to roar,
searching for its apogee, just months ahead. St. Petersburg
has been named "the healthiest spot on the face of the earth"
by the AMA. Its new Million Dollar Pier is about to open. In
Miami, streets are choked with cars . . . in the middle of the
night! The city is filled with real-estate people, men in knickers, and touring cars with mattresses strapped to the roofs.
Hustlers are shanghaiing passersby into buying land. Office
buildings and hotels rise out of swampland . . . a land frenzy
unlike anything America has ever seen.

Joseph Young's white "Hollywood Busses" bring people in
from the Northeast and Midwest, creating excitement as they
roll along filled with happy folks going to Florida! Salesmen
and "closers" are also on board, hustling the folks as they
travel. Caravans of busses are delivering prospects to the giant, empty gates dotting the landscape.

But what about those hurricanes? Young's prospects are
told the great news that Hollywood could never be damaged
by a hurricane because (are your ready?) "this area is pro-
tected by the Gulf Stream," the gently flowing "river-in-the-
ocean," which will turn away any hurricane! (And remember,
if you'll buy that, we still have that land in the Everglades we
want to talk with you about.)

The *St. Petersburg Times* ran over twenty-five million lines of ads during 1925, much in real estate, and still placed second to *The Miami Herald,* which set a world record in advertising with over forty-two million lines of ads, much also in real estate, all largely fueled by the raging land boom.

Land sales would still go hopping along; construction would still be OK. Tampa streets are choked with boomers; Highways 27, 19, 441, 41, and 1 are all busy with traffic flowing south; inland towns are enjoying newfound prosperity; St. Pete's downtown sidewalks are jammed with visitors, with kids stepping out into the street to get through the crowds. "Boomers" are everywhere looking for action. Even reports of an oil strike in Oldsmar fail to excite folks. There's really just too much goin' on. Who has time for an oil strike, anyway? It's probably just a promotional gimmick.

Land sales begin to peak in late 1925. The boom continues, but slows from its breakneck pace of the previous forty-eight months. Few take notice. The steam was gradually seeping from the massive engine and boiler, which had been "cooking" in Florida for nearly a decade.

THE SLIDE (ALSO THE TEETER-TOTTER AND THE DUNK-TANK)

To insiders, it was becoming more clear with each passing week that the boom was slowly losing steam. That which had soared so effortlessly over the previous five years, creating instant millionaires from doormen, car-parkers, hairdressers, countless Binder Boys, and other happy hustlers, was gently slowing in its path.

The "little people" could not have known of this. They remained steadfast in the certainty that the boom could only continue as it had . . . going straight up!

By 1925, Fantasy-land was beginning to crinkle just a tiny bit around the edges, but crinkle it did. The IRS began to follow up on large real-estate deals, demanding immediate cash tax-payment. Cash?? Why, no one uses cash! This is the boom!

Now, unexpectedly, another Grinch comes on the scene. A whole lot of people suddenly realize that the only way to bring nails, hammers, boards, workers, you name it, from up

North down to the beating heart of the boom, at least in Miami, is via the Florida East Coast Railway. And it only has one track!

The only other way to get supplies at all is by ship, down the Atlantic seaboard, through the Miami inlet to builders waiting on the docks. That's it!

Now the FEC, enjoying the happy burden of an unbelievable amount of freight-billing for over five years, finds it's running out of freight cars! It discovers about a thousand cars backed up on rail sidings in Jacksonville, waiting to get on the single southbound track; it finds another thousand or so on sidings somewhere along the route leading downstate, and another thousand or so, sitting on sidings in Miami, still filled with freight! It was now discovered that freight consignees, lacking warehouse space, were simply leaving their goods in the freight cars, using them as temporary warehouses until they "could get around to unloading them."

The FEC, at one point, estimated it was missing some seven thousand freight cars, which were sitting around on rail sidings in one location or another. Probably their computer was down. (Remember, a 1925 computer was a guy in old dungarees—you remember dungarees—with a clipboard and a big wax crayon, walking along the siding, counting boxcars.)

At this point, the FEC, lifeline of the boom, for whatever reasons declared an embargo on all shipments going to South Florida, except medical supplies, high-priority goods, perishables, and foodstuffs. At the same time, the FEC realized it would have to upgrade its rails into a dual-track system, and began construction.

For now, the only means of transporting millions of tons of supplies for builders in South Florida is via boat, down the coast. The largest ships are laden with construction material—the ocean-shipping business probably never had it so good—and the boom is happily rolling along.

Ships lie at anchor outside Biscayne Bay, awaiting their turn to enter the harbor. Things seems to be going along swimmingly. After all, it is January 26, in a brand-new year of 1926, and everything looks great for the coming year. But remember, behind every silver lining, there's a big black cloud. Florida's fabulous boom is about to be dealt, not a "one-two" punch, but a one-two-three-four-five-six punch! Watch.

It's January 26, 1926, and the largest sailing vessel ever to try to enter Biscayne Bay is sailing through its channel, to be converted into a 100-room, floating hotel. It is the *Prinz Valdemar,* sailing slowly in strong, gusting winds through the confines of what one day will be Government Cut.

The whipping, Atlantic winds catch her sails; the *Valdemar* begins, slowly, horrifyingly, to roll over and settles slowly on the bottom of the channel . . . in the center of the only access to the harbor and port from open sea.

At that moment, some one hundred ships lie at anchor outside the port, all loaded with supplies, carrying over forty million board feet of lumber alone for builders who were facing customers, waiting for their new Florida homes.

Engineers had to dig a channel around the vessel to move it—a month's work—while developers, contractors, salesmen, and carpenters watched their excitement grind slowly to a crawl, for want of a nail. Builders were unable to deliver for their customers, yet credit lines had to be serviced, bank loans paid, and workmen provided for. It was a generation before the "catch-22" phrase became a part of our language, but that was exactly where the land boom found itself in January 1926.

"People traffic" had reached such levels in mid-1925 that the FEC estimated some twenty-five hundred new people were arriving in South Florida alone every day, with over a thousand of these holding only one-way tickets. They had come to Florida to stay.

By this time, some banks were literally forced to foreclose on some loans, partial developments, even small houses for which they had absolutely no use, and really didn't want.

Builders crept into bankruptcy. Some simply "walked," leaving their projects and investments behind.

People continued to pour into Florida. In August 1925, many stories told of Northern post offices receiving countless change-of-address requests, indicating a move to Florida. Savannah was said to have received over six thousand requests in one month.

The boom continued to creep along, weathering thus far a solid "one-two punch," the *Valdemar* sinking and the FEC freight embargo.

Suddenly, it is summer 1926.

The Prinz Valdemar capsized while entering Biscayne Bay on January 26, 1926, and sank to the bottom, forcing the land boom to pause and catch its breath. (Courtesy Florida State Photographic Archives)

The winter of 1925-26 was the worst freeze since the 1893-94 "Great Freeze," which brought Flagler's rails to Miami in the first place. Its record was to last nearly seventy years until the Great Freeze of 1989-90.

Following the bitter cold, Florida's 1926 summer was a "burner," with stifling heat records set daily. Even the brand-new ice machine invented by Dr. John Gorrie in Apalachicola, and his resulting "air-conditioning" apparatus, did little to ease the '26 scorcher. There was almost an ominous feeling in the intensity of the 1926 summer.

And suddenly, Florida is looking directly down the barrel of hurricane season! June and July pass. August is an oven. And it's September 17, 1926.

Florida has not seen a major hurricane since 1910 . . . for sixteen years! During that time, Southeast Florida alone has seen a population growth of up to 500 percent each year. Most of the population knows nothing of storms, exactly replicating the situation in the 1990s, seventy years later.

All construction was being done by persons with little or no knowledge of Florida storms. There was no zoning; there were only "boomtime builders." Building codes did not reflect concern for hurricanes, since there hadn't been one since 1910.

In that great school of experience (the one where you get to take the test before you take the lesson), investors were nearly always startled to find the incredible role in Florida history played by—of all things—the weather! It can change all the spots on the dice, all the cards in the hand, and all the rules of the game, with a single "blow."

In 1926, there was no National Hurricane Center, no hurricane watch or warning system to speak of, few storm warnings, and no cute names. The news of a storm was simply passed from town to town by local weather-bureau people. Rising seas were noted by coastal towns, but still would take many by surprise.

Florida depression kids saw storms as two things: A) A chance to stay home from school. B) A chance to dig holes in the empty lot next door and watch them fill up with water. Things were different.

THE THREE-FOUR PUNCH

On September 17, 1926, a major hurricane hit smack-dab in the middle of Miami, driving a small nail into the eventual coffin of the boom. Marjory Stoneman Douglas, in her epic chronology, *The Everglades: River of Grass,* told of the 1926 storm exploding as a giant bomb, only exploding all night long, 125-mile-an-hour winds shrieking through the night and driving boats into houses, ships aground, and tides up into the streets. South Florida was about to have its own crash three years before the rest of the nation.

The storm wrecked half-built buildings, forever changing the skyline of Miami. One fourteen-story building under construction was immediately changed to a seven-story structure. Nearly four hundred lives were lost. Investors suddenly paused in their dash for profits and sales to look over their collective shoulders and inquire, "What's this?"

By fall 1926, after the massive hurricane cleanup, an astonishing fact became apparent. The boom had such incredible momentum that even a storm taking almost four hundred lives only brought a pause in its drive. It broke stride, struggled back to its knees, and continued to move, albeit at a slower pace.

Buildings were still going up in areas away from the massive storm: the new Breakers Hotel in Palm Beach (the third Breakers—the first two had been destroyed by fire) along with other Flagler/FEC hotels, the new Casa Marina in Key West, the Park Plaza in Winter Park, and beautiful structures in Venice, Sarasota, Tampa, and St. Petersburg.

The '26 blow, with 392 persons killed, 7,000 injured, and 17,000 made homeless, did frightening damage to small towns, such as Moore Haven, where a wall of water roared through the tiny Lake Okeechobee hamlet. And yet, the Tampa Bay area and parts of the Gulf Coast did not feel the brunt of the storm itself. Instead, they actually experienced a "miniboom" as visitors came to these areas instead of the lower east coast.

The boom struggled through the remainder of 1926, cleaning up the debris after the killer storm, reorganizing, and refinancing its way through the 1927 spring and summer season, helped by a strong tourist trade that carried it all the way to spring and summer 1928. And, once again, suddenly it's September—September 1928!

For those who thought the '26 hurricane to be a bad blow, with its nearly four hundred deaths, the 1928 blow with an estimated three thousand deaths was the final straw. Winds up to 160 miles per hour brought a twelve- to sixteen-foot wall of water, opening an area from West Palm Beach to Lake Okeechobee as it surged through the streets of the coastal city. It is well within the memory of area residents, including eminent historian Judge Jim Knott, to whom we are indebted for his personal remembrances of Florida history.

In Lake Okeechobee settlements, almost two thousand were killed; another thousand unaccounted for. Migrant workers were swept out into the saw-grass swamps, with bodies unearthed years later by workmen plowing or clearing the land. Through the inky blackness of the night, people clung to anything as entire houses were washed away. Over a thousand people drowned within one hour's time.

The '28 blow is rated the third worst disaster in U.S. history, following the Johnstown Flood and Galveston hurricane, and is by far the worst storm in Florida history.

It is the fourth blow in the "one-two-three-four punch" aimed directly at Florida's gasping land boom.

Following the '28 blow, more investors simply "walk." Banks inherit more developments, e.g., the "mysterious" Lakewood Estates pine forests of St. Petersburg. For decades, private pilots, checking their charts, will find the word *grid*, accompanied by a tiny "tic-tac-toe" symbol, all over Florida, as navigational checkpoints. Looking down from 7,000 feet, the pilot sees glaring white, crisscrossing lines. They are streets laid out in a grid, carved in Florida's white sands, sometimes stretching for miles. Many of them are simply someone's dream, where a developer laid down his tools, laid off his workers, and walked away.

But the unbelievable land boom *still* tries to rise again, as developers attempt to recapture the magic. Paris Singer of the Palm Beaches backs Harry Kelsey in his dream of Kelsey City, later to become the town of Lake Park. Kelsey actually sold out to the Royal Palm Beach Land Company for $30 million, and his buyers took the impending body blow, the death of the boom, lurking just around the corner.

Kelsey's instincts were said to be better than his judgment. He died in the 1950s, having used up much of his fortune still promoting a retirement town west of Miami, where everything would be perfect.

Kelsey's name for his perfect town was—Utopia! Like the man who invented a soft drink called 6-Up, Kelsey never realized how close he came to immortality.

The '28 storm passed. Florida cleaned up its mess, buried its dead, and burned bodies to prevent epidemic. The state had now been dealt four body blows, any one of which would have been sufficient to stop a lesser giant in its tracks: the *Valdemar* sinking, the FEC freight embargo, the '26 blow, and the '28 superblow, all within a period of thirty-six months. While Florida was reeling, its land boom struggled to rise again. But the boom, like all America, found itself staring directly into the eyes of Tuesday, October 29, 1929: Black Tuesday! The Florida land boom was about to become history, but not without a fight, and not without at least one last bigger-than-all-the-rest binge, coming right up.

MIZNER MADNESS

With all the history, heartbreak, euphoria, and tears of the boom, with the "one-two-three-four-five-six punch" of the channel block, rail embargo, two killer hurricanes, the stock-market crash, and the national depression, Florida—in the midst of chaos—was *still* able to stir the hearts of investors and developers. As the ancient Greeks said, "It would take a tiny grain of madness," but it could be done. At the outset of 1926, as the boom began its slide, came that tiny grain of madness to be known as the Eccentric Mizner Brothers, and with them, the grandest single story of the Florida land boom, the Boca Raton Land Development Company.

Now, being "the grandest of them all" requires some documentation and credibility support. Let's take a look:

A) The development challenged the gods, created on the "downside of the mountain," facing two killer hurricanes and the madness that was to follow.

B) It encompassed 17,000 acres of prime, coastal land,

directly between Flagler's Palm Beaches and the boom's beating heart, Miami.

C) It was dreamed of, by its creators, as "the world's greatest resort"—not Florida's; not the U.S.'s; hey, the world's!

D) Its investors included names from internationally known American dynasties.

E) It was the dream of eccentric, architect, showman Addison Mizner, and his really eccentric brother, raconteur, wit, gambler, promoter, known hustler, Wilson Mizner.

F) And finally, it was promoted almost "after the ball was over" . . . the fat lady had already sung! They said it couldn't be done, but the Mizners went ahead and did it anyway.

G) And finally #2, even after it had gone through several death throes of its own, it created and became not one but three more legends within its own lifetime.

H) And really finally, it continues at this writing as one of America's premier resort hotels, probably unmatched on the continent.

That should suffice.

Addison Mizner was a man made for his times. He came to Florida, sickly, in 1918, almost exactly at the beginning of Florida's wild and crazy decade. His timing was perfect.

As a "sometimes-architect, enigma, mystery-man," his first venture was with his friend, Paris Singer. Together, they built what was to be a hospital for World War I veterans. The building was to overlook the balmy waters of Lake Worth on "Palm Beach Island."

As the war suddenly ended, they converted the building into a new idea—a private social club. The idea caught on, and that which became the Everglades Club also became the focal point for all the first society citizens of the island resort.

Soon Mizner was in demand, creating mansions for much of society on the fantasy island. Quickly, he became almost a cult figure. One simply had to have Mizner "do" one's Palm Beach house. He literally drew sketches on napkins at parties and turned the actual work over to assistants.

Within months, Mizner was caught up in his own dreams, creating mansion after mansion, the darling of society, in demand at every event, rubbing elbows with the rich and powerful. With this heady input, it was not long until Mizner determined to create his own city, his own jewel, his monument. And Mizner's Boca Raton Land Development Company was born.

With his personal "cult" at a peak in early 1924, Mizner was already beginning plans for his city. In April 1925, he announced plans to build a $6 million hotel as a centerpiece for his 17,000-acre planned city; it would include scenic canals, golf courses, wide boulevards, ocean property . . . truly a dream, the world's greatest!

The project enjoyed the attention of the cream of Palm Beach blue-chip investors: Vanderbilt, Singer, Wanamaker, DuPont, Irving Berlin, Elizabeth Arden, and others. Almost instantly, it became a success. Roads were jammed from Miami to West Palm Beach, with $2 million in lots sold on opening day alone.

The dream was to become the grandest venture of them all, set in the tiny village of Boca Raton, with probably fewer than six hundred persons in the whole town. It was also to become the most thundering downfall of any of the Florida dreams over the golden decade of the boom.

During 1925, Mizner continued to build his hotel, the Cloisters Inn. He added a 160-foot-wide boulevard, Camino Real, the Road of Kings, which ran only from the Mizner train station, past the Mizner construction office, to the Mizner hotel. The boulevard, at twenty cars wide the widest in America at the time, was to include a Venetian canal in its center, down which gondolas would bring guests from the train station to the hotel. At this reading, possibly some adopted Crackers, having wondered at the vast expanse of Camino Real, may learn of its original purpose.

The Mizners, in their flamboyant ad campaigns in Northern newspapers, declared simply: "I am Boca Raton! The Greatest Resort in the World!" This headline was referring to a tiny cluster of houses, construction shacks, a little train station, some nondescript gravel roads, and miles of vacant land filled with weeds, ants, and sandspurs.

Addison brought in brother Wilson to handle sales, promotion, costs, and dollars, while he concentrated on building plans. Wilson was to tend to the business end, or so investors thought.

This original map of Boca Raton from February 1924 lets the reader discern "where everything is" today. The Mizner hotel is not yet on the map, and along the FEC tracks is "Dixie Highway," from left to right. At the fork, the eastern road is labeled "New Dixie Highway." (Courtesy Florida State Photographic Archives)

Land sales soared; $26 million within 120 days. The Mizners were said to be holding $10 million in down payments, while they were spending some $200 million in backers' funds, including T. Coleman DuPont and Charles G. Dawes, then vice-president of the nation.

The Cloisters opens February 1, 1926! The event rivals any movie premiere of the time. Famous names from national society abound. But back in the shadows, the boom is slowing. And September 1926 is just around the corner.

As the boom hesitated, land sales faltered. Payments slowed. Mizner, as the prototype of all Florida promoters, an entire "Binder-Boys" system rolled into one man, still had to maintain his bank-debt service and had to meet monstrous bank loans.

At this point, with sales slowing and the Northern press bombarding the boom with damaging editorials and stories about dubious sales techniques and outrageous claims by Florida developers, Wilson Mizner decided to counterattack. Mizner began to run ads including the lines, "Attach this ad to your land contract. It will become a part of your contract and prove that we are personally guaranteeing every statement in the ad to be absolutely true!"

Quickly, some of the major names among the investors, apparently with concern for their personal liability, decided to withdraw from the venture. The enormity of the project was such that their withdrawal did not take place in the usual manner; simply a letter to the directors. Instead, the principals placed a public letter in an ad in New York newspapers, stating their resignation publicly and their complete disassociation with the Boca Raton project. The ad gave immense concern to potential buyers, and marked the beginning of the end for Mizner's dream.

As sales and cash flow slowed, creditors began to press for their payments. Irate buyers learned for the first time that the brothers actually had no money of their own, that many statements were simply wild promises, that many planned improvements were not to be, and that the entire dream had been done on borrowed money. Mizner was to learn now an old Cracker gem, "Ain't nothin' wrong with runnin' into debt; it's runnin' into creditors that gives you trouble."

By fall 1926, Mizner was forced to give up the Cloisters Inn, turning over the reins to Dawes and a Chicago investor group. The group sold the entire project to Indiana's "farm boy," Clarence Geist, who was to operate the hotel as his own fiefdom until he died.

The incredible structure of the hotel, even today, bears the stamp of the genius of Mizner. As you walk the great stone halls and dance on a ballroom floor constructed over an indoor swimming pool, you can envision Mizner pounding fake antique holes in beams and blocks of stone to "age" them, chipping fireplace mantels, beating floors, even "forgetting" to add stairs to a mansion, to see if the client was paying attention, then adding the stairs up the outside of the structure.

And the third brother teamed up with Wilson to scrounge spare building material with which to build a tiny church, so his mother might be able to attend services conducted by him. He was a shy, quiet, retiring priest. As we recall, Adam and Eve had a third son who got into no trouble at all, so we never hear about him.

During the waning days of the boom, matching the close of the "Mizner Period" of Florida, investment bankers in the North drafted "blue-sky" laws, indirectly aimed at the boom. In one savings bank, 100,000 depositors had withdrawn $20 million in deposits, apparently for land speculation in Florida.

One report summed it up succinctly: "If all the Florida real estate lots were actually going to be occupied by buyers in 1925, one-half the entire population of the country would have had to move to Florida." If so, there would have been an Addison Mizner, and a whole bunch of Binder Boys, to help them get settled. And the Florida land boom would probably still be going on as you read these lines.

As a whole bunch of big operators found out, there's one thing about being poor. It's inexpensive.

IT'S A SHAME THE DEPRESSION CAME ALONG JUST WHEN EVERYBODY WAS OUT OF WORK

And so, the land boom died completely, wiping out the previous years of soaring prices, armies of hustlers and promoters, fortunes, dreams that soared, dreams that soured, and dreams that crashed and burned on the rocks. It faded to become a fleeting memory in Florida's economic story, the state's "first quarter earnings" of the twentieth century. It was an historic experience, an emotional one, a philosophical display of raw human nature and greed on the grandest of scales, by both the great and the small. It was a travelling sideshow, a carnival barker, a snake-oil salesman . . . all rolled into one.

When buyers can be told—and will believe—that the city of Hollywood-by-the-Sea will never be hit by hurricanes because the ocean's Gulf Stream will make the storm turn away, this ranks alongside America's innocents letting an entire nation go to war, sailing from Tampa, motivated by hundreds of newspaper atrocity stories. When buyers can be lulled into purchasing lots they've never seen, the boom must rank with all the major hustles of all time. And when—as pointed out—a single promotion can be so immense it would require half the population of the nation to move to fulfill its purpose, it would have resulted at the time in a Florida population of some thirty million people in 1930.

By 2020, in the "Tomorrow" chapter up ahead, we will probably have all those people in the Sunshine State. And we may start another land boom all over again. If we do, we'll get all kinds of folks: hustlers, promoters, card-sharks, "boomers," and all the rest. 'Cause just as the old Cracker axiom says, "A lot of folks settled down, down South, 'cause they didn't settle up, up North."

SPECIAL FLORIDA LAND BOOM
CREDITS AND ACKNOWLEDGMENTS

In delving into a project of such scope as the Florida land boom—encompassing fifty years of developing and ten years of soaring—we are deeply indebted to chroniclers of various areas who've undertaken detailed research into specific transactions, dollars, incidents, and personalities. We thank:

Raymond Arsenault, for his exhaustive work in *St. Petersburg and the Florida Dream,* which brings up details not even included in this author's childhood memories of the streets of the Sunshine City.

Gene Burnett, for all his *Florida Trend* columns and his fine work in *Florida's Past.*

Seth Bramson, whose *Speedway to Sunshine,* the story of Flagler's FEC rails, is probably the most in-depth study of any railroad, anywhere, anytime.

Hampton Dunn, originator of the *Yesterday's* series, and his eighteen books on Florida as only a Floral City native son could possibly know her.

Judge Jim Knott, for his in-depth coverage in the *Yesterday's Palm Beach* series, with delightful stories of Fantasy Land.

Stuart McIver, for his outstanding documentation of Ft. Lauderdale, Broward County, and Southeast Florida in his *Glimpses of South Florida History* and *Yesterday's Palm Beaches.*

And old friend Nixon Smiley, with his scholarly work in *Yesterday's Florida.* We hope this particular section will serve as a small memorial to this gentle man, his fine, friendly writing, and his love for Florida.

We cannot recommend too highly all the research and work created by these writers, nor the vast library of Florida information maintained by Sam Mickler at his distribution center, Mickler's Floridiana, the largest book distribution center in the world with only one subject. If you want material on Florida, Sam is the man, and Mickler's Floridiana of Oviedo, Florida, near Orlando, is the place.

CHAPTER 7

Florida Firsts

FLORIDA'S MOST AND LEAST

One of the easiest ways to absorb information is to go through your ABCs. These ABCs will spotlight the old Cracker mind-set which has helped create the Magic Land.

At the Osceola Historical Society in Kissimmee, our favorite Maine transplant, Elinor Perrin, says there is an old "Down-Easter" saying that goes, "Springtime in the state of Maine is mainly a state of mind." So is high season in Palm Beach. So is being a Cracker *at all!*

In this section of your Florida ABCs, some may be simple, some more difficult, but all belong in the homework of any serious Cracker or would-be Cracker. In the following pages, we'll bring you the answers. So here we go. Work your way through some ABCs, and have a nice trip. (There may be 976,384 facts in this section alone, but who's counting?)

A is for A _ _ _ _ _ I _ _ _ _ _: Charming, laid-back, old Florida, in the northeast corner pocket area. Served under eight flags, more than any other place on the continent. Was even the capital of the East Florida Republic—its own country! How about that!

B is for B _ _ _ _ H _ _ _ _ Bridge: The largest, longest continuous bridge in Florida.

203

B is for B _ _ _ _ _ : Would you believe, in 1837, with Florida teetering on the edge of bankruptcy and owing every bank, the legislature made it illegal for one of these to run for or hold any public office in the state?

B is for B _ _ _ _ I _ _ _ _ _ _ _ _ : Heaviest natural wood in existence. Native to Florida. Cubic foot can weigh eighty pounds. Used for propellers in WWII. Harder than steel!

B is for B _ _ _ _ _ _ _ : Name of Britain's famed speed car. Set world records on the sand at Daytona Beach.

B is for B _ _ T _ _ _ _ : Famed "Singing Tower," home to the world's largest flamingo. When he eats, he turns his head upside down.

C is for C _ _ _ C _ _ _ _ _ _ _ _ _ : The first name given to the continent by Ponce de Leon, along with La Florida.

C is for C _ _ _ _ _ _ _ _ _ : "The Sweetest Town in the U.S."

C is for C _ _ _ _ -F _ _ _ _ _ _ B _ _ _ _ C _ _ _ _ : The world's grandest political football.

D is for D _ _ _ _ _ _ _ B _ _ _ _ : "The World's Most Famous Beach," where all the speed records we could ever need have been set.

D is for D _ S _ _ _ , Hernando: Found the Mississippi River, starting his search in Tampa Bay. With a priest along, celebrated the New World's first Christmas in 1539.

D is for D _ _ _ _ _ : "The World's Luckiest Fishing Village."

E is for E _ _ _ _ _ F _ _ _ _ _ _ _ _ of L _ _ _ _ : The longest nighttime parade in the world.

E is for E _ _ _ _ F _ _ _ _ : The world's largest air force installation.

E is for E _ _ _ _ _ _ _ _ _ _ : The world's most unusual "river."

F is for F _ _ _ : A type of car that set records at Daytona.

F is for F _ . L _ _ _ _ _ _ _ _ _ _ : Home of the world's first hurricane-proof hostelry.

F is for F _ . M _ _ _ _ : The adopted home of Thomas Edison, along with his prefab home and his swimming pool — two firsts.

G is for G _ _ _ _ _ _ _ _ _ , John: Brought America's first golf course to Florida.

G is for G _ _ _ _ _ _ _ _ _ _ : A big yellow citrus fruit that Florida introduced to the New World.

H is for H _ _ _ _ _ -core concrete block: The world's first one was developed in Florida.

H is for H _ _ _ _ _ : Florida leads the nation in the production of this item.

I is for I _ _ -making machine: Invented in Florida.

J is for J _ _ _ _ _ _ _ _ _ _ _ _ : One of the world's largest city areas.

J is for J _ _ _ Pennekamp Underwater Park: You can see forty-one varieties of living coral rock at this place in the Keys. It is unique in the hemisphere.

K is for K _ _ W _ _ _ : America's southernmost city.

K is for K _ _ _ _ _ Club: The nation's original dog-racing track.

K is for K _ _ _ O _ _ _ _ _ J _ _ _ _ _ _ _ : The name given to the Orange Bowl celebration in Miami, which also includes one of the world's longest nighttime parades.

K is for K _ _ _ _ _ _ : The world's smallest citrus fruit.

L is for L _ F _ _ _ _ _ _ : The first name given to any land in the New World.

L is for L _ _ _ _ _ _ _ _ _ : Florida has been acclaimed as the world capital for this weather phenomenon.

M is for "M _ _ _ H _ _ a L _ _ _ _ _ L _ _ _ ": The world's first recorded song.

M is for M _ _ _ , Dr. Samuel: One of only two persons ever held at Ft. Jefferson, Dry Tortugas.

M is for M _ _ _ train: One of the first trains in the world pulled by this animal was in Florida.

N is for N _ _ _ _ _ _ _ Hurricane Center: The leading hurricane center in the world.

N is for N _ _ P _ _ _ R _ _ _ _ _ : Site of the word's largest annual barbecue.

O is for O _ _ _ _ _ _ : Three-fourths of America's supply of these fruits come from Florida.

O is for O _ _ _ _ _ : Homestead, Dade County, is said to have the world's largest collection of this flower.

P is for P _ _ _ _ _ _ : The bass-fishing capital of the world.

P is for P _ _ _ _ _ _ _ _ _ : The world's largest naval air station.

P is for P _ _ _ _ _ _ , Dr. John: He brought us limes, lemons, and avocados.

P is for P _ _ _ of M _ _ _ _ : The world's leading cruise-ship port.

P is for P _ _ _ _ _   L _ _ _ _ _ _ : The world's oldest one is in St. Augustine.

S is for S _ _ _ _ _ _ _ : Stuart is the world capital for this.

S is for S _ . A _ _ _ _ _ _ _ _ _ : Once and for all, the oldest continuously occupied site in North America.

S is for S _ . A _ _ _ _ _ _ _ _ _   G _ _ _ _ : Florida's favorite crabgrass.

S is for S _ . J _ _ _ _ : This is one of the earth's five rivers that flow northward.

S is for S _ . P _ _ _ _ _ _ _ _ _ _ : "The Healthiest Spot on Earth," according to the AMA in 1885. Also the birthplace of commercial aviation.

S is for S _ _ _ _ _ _ _ _ : The first factory of this kind was in Florida.

S is for S _ _ _ _ _ _ _ _   I _ _ _ _ _   W _ _ _ : The longest state of hostilities known to man.

S is for S _ _ _ _ : The first whale born in captivity.

S is for S _ _ _ _ _   S _ _ _ _ _ _ : The world's largest springs.

T is for T _ _ _ _ : This city is the world's cigar-making capital, producing over a fifth of all cigars smoked in the U.S.

T is for T _ _ _ _ _ _ _ _ : This fruit was developed in Florida.

T is for T _ _ _ _ _ : Florida's largest single money crop.

V   is   for   V _ _ _ _ _ _   A _ _ _ _ _ _ _ B _ _ _ _ _ _ _ : This incredible structure at the Space Center encompasses about a half-billion cubic feet. It's where they assemble the space vehicle and is largest single structure on Earth.

V is for V _ _ _ _ _ : Charming town founded by and specifically for members of the Brotherhood of Locomotive

Engineers. Fortunately, today, they let other people live there, too.

W is for W _ _ _ _ _ _ S _ _ _ _ _ _ : Said to be the world's deepest natural springs, clearly viewable down 200 feet. Pours about billion gallons of water every day.

W is for W _ _ _ _ P_ _ _ _ _ _ _ _ _ _ C_ _ _ _ _ _ _ _ _ _ _ _ _ : Near Zephyrhills, these are the world championships for this incredible jumping sport.

Z is for Z _ _ _ _ _ _ _ T _ _ _ _ _ : This famous officer, on Florida duty, met, courted, and married a charming Alabama miss, who later became America's First Lady in The White House (creating an awkward situation at family dinners, since her father was also president of the Confederate States of America). (It's always tough to come up with a Z.)

So there you have just a few of Florida's first and last, worst and best, most and least, west and east. We could have added in her first drive-in restaurant. Their slogan was, "Come as you are—but stay in the car." But we'll have a lot more just ahead, mixed in with some of the answers.

Incidentally, trying to cover *all* of Florida's claims would be like saying the Empire State Building was designed to give the illusion of height. We hope we didn't miss one near and dear to your heart, but maybe it'll turn up ahead a piece.

EXPERIENCE IS THE BEST TEACHER, AND YOU GET INDIVIDUAL INSTRUCTION

Now that you have just a few of Florida's claims, let's review the items and see how well you scored. We could have included Florida's first recipe for its famous depression sponge cake, which started out, "First you borrow all the ingredients. . . ." And there is no truth to the story that Tom Edison discovered a cure for which there is no disease, either. We stick to documented stuff, boy.

The *A* is delightful Amelia Island, with its town of Fernandina Beach, which lived under eight flags, more than any other place on the continent.

The largest, longest continuous bridge in Florida is the Bahia Honda Bridge. Folks usually just call it "Seven-Mile Bridge," and the real "folks" just call it "Seven-Mile."

In 1837—are you ready?—the legislature passed a bill making it illegal for any public office to be held by—a banker! (There's gotta be a heckuva story in there somewhere.) They even made it illegal for the state to—ready?—go into debt. Apparently they weren't getting along too well with the banks in 1837.

The next *B* is pretty tough too. It's black ironwood. And, speaking of wood, one-half of Florida is covered with forests.

And Britain's famous race car was the Bluebird, driven by Sir Malcolm Campbell. It set many of the major speed records on Daytona Beach.

That "Singing Tower" is Bok Tower, created by Edward W. Bok and home to the world's largest flamingo.

Cape Canaveral was the other "first name" given to the continent by Ponce de Leon, along with La Florida, and Clewiston is "The Sweetest Town in the U.S."

The world's grandest political football, the Cross-Florida Barge Canal, started and stopped on a fairly regular basis since old Tom Jefferson's day, and maybe since Menendez' day.

Under *D,* all the speed records we could ever need have been set at Daytona Beach, of course, "The World's Most Famous Beach."

And, as all school kids know, Hernando de Soto found the Mississippi River, but he started looking for it in Tampa Bay. That other *D* was the town of Destin, called "The World's Luckiest Fishing Village." Check it out.

The Edison Festival of Light says it's an even longer nighttime parade than the Orange Bowl Jamboree, which comes up just ahead. At any rate, Florida must have the first and second longest nighttime parades in the world—one for each coast.

And Eglin Field is also home to the world-famed Blue Angels Precision Flying Team, along with being the world's largest air force installation (third-of-a-billion acres).

That 2,746-square-mile "river"—the world's most unusual—is the Everglades, called "River of Grass" by famed writer Marjory Stoneman Douglas. It averages a width of 40-50 miles and a depth of six inches. Now that's a river.

The Fiat was a huge race car, nicknamed Mephistopheles, that set records at Daytona.

The world's first hurricane-proof hostelry was built in 1905 in Ft. Lauderdale: The New River Inn. First ever.

And, of course, Ft. Myers was the adopted home of Thomas Edison, along with his first prefab home construction, his first swimming pool, his goldenrod experiments to produce synthetic rubber, and his incandescent electric lights, which are still burning in his Ft. Myers home. It's a good thing Edison invented the electric light, or we'd all be watching TV by candlelight.

Hey, here's one for you! America's first golf course was brought to these shores in 1886 by Scot John Gillespie so he could enjoy his favorite game from Scotland. He brought it to Sarasota and America took a liking to it.

Of course, that big yellow citrus fruit is grapefruit. Florida introduced the biggie to the New World.

The first *H* is the world's first hollow-core concrete block, developed by Thomas King of Ft. Lauderdale during the land boom. It was easier for workers to work with and carry. (Sorry about that. We felt you needed a little challenge, and wanted to see if you were paying attention.)

But the other *H* is easy—it's honey. Florida leads the nation in production of it (along with the bees, of course).

Now, if you've been reading along at all, you know about Dr. John Gorrie. One of the world's unsung heroes, he developed the first ice-making machine, and first air-conditioning system. It was in Apalachicola and the man deserves a little more of our applause than he has gotten.

Jacksonville, annexing itself out to the county line, has become one of the world's largest city areas. And John Pennekamp Underwater Park is where you can see all that coral.

Of course, Key West is America's southernmost city. It was bought by John Simonton for $2,000 (that was for the whole island). And St. Petersburg's Kennel Club turns out to be the nation's original dog-racing track.

The King Orange Jamboree is the moniker given to the entire Orange Bowl celebration in Miami, including either the

Jacksonville, the Gateway City, in addition to producing eleven governors of Florida and becoming the City of Governors, annexed the entire county of Duval, becoming the largest city in land mass in the world. (Photo by Judy Jacobsen Photographic Service, Jacksonville)

world's longest or second-longest nighttime parade. (See Edison Festival of Light.)

W. C. Fields did about ten minutes on nothing but the spelling of the world's smallest citrus fruit, kumquat, or maybe it was cumquat.

By now you know the first name given to any land in the New World is La Florida, by Ponce back in 1513. We understand there is not much chance that our country will change its name to the United States of Florida, but that's what it probably should be.

But did you know, because of all her storms, Florida has also been acclaimed as the Lightning Capital of the World?

Hey, did you get the first *M*? None other than old Tom Edison and His Five Kilowatts (actually he didn't have a backup group, and he hadn't invented kilowatts yet, anyway) cut the world's first "platter." Tom sang the song on his home-recording cylinder, in his first successful attempt to capture sound. The song was "Mary Had a Little Lamb." It didn't sell too well. He probably should have had a backup group.

Dr. Samuel Mudd was one of only two persons ever held at Ft. Jefferson, Dry Tortugas. He was the doctor who set John Wilkes Booth's leg.

One of the world's first mule trains ran from Tallahassee to St. Marks in 1824. An old mule pulled a flatcar along some wooden rails.

The National Hurricane Center in Miami is the leading hurricane center in the world. It is a great friend in times of need. And the site of the world's largest annual barbecue is the town of New Port Richey, north of Clearwater.

That first *O* could only be oranges.

That next *O* is for orchid.

The world's bass-fishing capital is Palatka, the charming old lumber town on the St. Johns River.

That second *P* can only be Pensacola, with the world's largest naval air station.

The good doctor who brought us limes, lemons, and avocados was Dr. Perrine, whose town, south of Miami, commemorates his name. The Port of Miami has become the

Early roads in the "real" historical parts of Florida include this "Main Street" of Old St. Augustine. The City Gates, dating from the seventeenth century, retain their original charm in this 1900 print. (Courtesy Florida State Photographic Archives)

Florida's relationship with air and sea grew into outer space. The massive Vehicle Assembly Building (VAB) is the largest enclosed space on Earth. A Titan III is lifting off from the launch pad in the background. (Courtesy Florida State Photographic Archives, NASA, and the U.S. Air Force Eastern Test Range Photo Laboratory)

world's leading cruise-ship port with its fantastic facility. And that last *P,* in St. Augustine, is the world's oldest public library.

The "Sailfish Capital of the World" is lovely Stuart, on the Treasure Coast. And, once and for all, St. Augustine is the oldest continuously occupied site in North America. That crabgrass you thought you left up North is Florida's favorite, St. Augustine grass. It works great in sand and sun. The St. Johns River is the giant that flows northward along with Earth's four other unique rivers. A couple of the others are the Nile and the Amazon. We can't remember the others. Write if you think of them.

And that "Healthiest Spot on Earth" was St. Petersburg! It was also the town that, almost literally, forgot its role as the birthplace of commercial aviation until city fathers accidentally stumbled across the fact in planning the city's anniversary. They had old records checked, and "by golly, we were first in the world; how 'bout that?" That first passenger-carrying airline flight was January 1, 1914.

The next *S* was the first saltworks, developed by soldiers to get salt out of the water, so they could use the salt. Tomorrow it may be the other way around.

The longest state of hostilities of mankind were the Seminole Indian Wars, finally settled 134 years after the last skirmishes, with the treaty being ratified in 1976.

The other *S* items include Shamu, the first whale born in captivity, and Silver Springs, the world's largest, pouring us about a billion gallons of pure, spring water everyday.

Tampa, of course, is the world's cigar-making capital. The tangerine was first developed in Brooksville, but the tomato is Florida's largest single money crop.

Surely you got that first *V* . . . it's pretty hard to miss. It's the largest thing of its kind on Earth. It's the Vehicle Assembly Building.

That "locomotive engineers' town" turned out to be charming Venice on the Gulf.

Fabulous Wakulla Springs is Florida's "other" giant springs. And that "jumping sport" competition turns out to be the World Parachuting Championships. Just testing.

Under *Z,* it was young Maj. Zachary Taylor who married the daughter of Jefferson Davis. It marked the first—and the last—time that presidents of two combative nations, in this

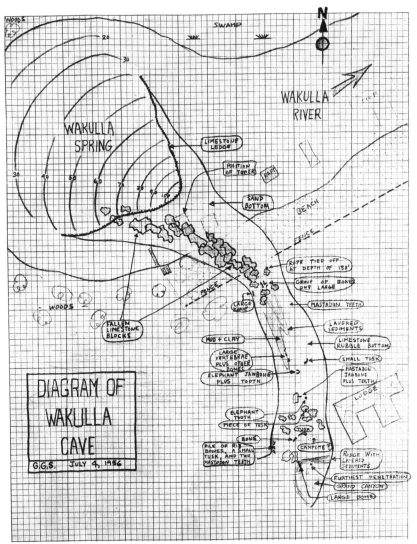

This incredible sketch of Wakulla Springs, the world's deepest, shows that a rope was tied off at a depth of 180 feet, yet diver exploration indicated as much as another 100 feet beyond, with finds including bones, tusks, even a campsite. (Courtesy Florida State University)

case, the United States of America and the Confederate States of America, were in-laws. Fortunately for the kids, it wasn't actually during the war, but it might have been awkward at family reunions.

REMEMBER—FLORIDA EVEN GETS THE SUN BEFORE CALIFORNIA

There you have a quick trip through some Florida firsts. Listen, don't talk bad about these little numbers. We could have included the world's first airplane catapult from a ship in Pensacola in 1914, but we didn't. We could have worked in the Franciscan Friars teaching school, in St. Augustine in 1569, but you'd never have gotten F _ _ _ _ _ _ _ _ _ F _ _ _ _ _, now would you?

Hey, we could have hit you with the world's largest commercial seaplane base, in Miami, where we got to see the Pan American Flying Boats and all that, but we didn't.

And we didn't even bring up the Swamp Cabbage Festival in La Belle. Or we could have brought up Dr. Gorrie's miracle cure for the common cough in 1845. It was two tablespoons of castor oil and man, you didn't dare cough. We didn't bring that up.

We could have brought in reams of stuff about Florida's space-shots, like it cost $2 billion for that trip to the moon. Of course that included meals. And we could've gone into Lake Worth's famous National Horseshoe Pitching Championships. Or if you really want to get historical, how about the first clay vessels in the U.S. produced by pre-Columbian Indians in Florida, predating the rest of the U.S. by a thousand years or so?

See? You really got off easy. Next time, we won't be so gentle.

Or how about those two guys who drove that brand new LaSalle all the way to Key West across the railroad ties, just to show how smooth the ride was? Never did hear what became of the car. It was a Florida first!

And, for that matter, Florida invented draft-protestors in 1942. They were called "soldiers." She was also first to develop frozen orange juice. In 1893-94, you got it right off the

By the 1930s, these Pan American Airways Sikorsky Flying Boats developed vital links between the economies of the U.S., South America, and the islands, as well as serving as training planes for World War II flight crews. This became the famed Caribbean Clipper. Thought by some to appear ungainly at rest in the water, the plane became beautifully sleek in flight, here over a 1930 Miami skyline. The new "Skyscraper Jail," pyramided top floors of the courthouse building, is at the far right. (Courtesy Florida State Photographic Archives)

trees. She renewed the patent in 1989-90. It's also the place where our beloved Snowbirds come every February to hear the little birds coughing in the trees.

One very small town developed the nation's first one-way street. It worked fine, until they realized they only had one street and had to drop the idea.

The Magic Land has had a lot of good folks over the past five hundred years or so. They've done a lot of good stuff, and we'll all have a ton of new folks doing their thing in Florida tomorrow, just ahead.

CHAPTER 8

Tomorrow

ONE THING ABOUT LIVING
IN THE PAST—IT'S CHEAPER

Some folks remember the bays. Florida's bays were beautiful: sun-drenched miles of open water by day, and moon-silvered by night. The state was ringed by beautiful bays, or inlets and rivers that were like open bays. Pensacola, Panama City, Apalachicola, Tampa, Sarasota, Ft. Myers, Biscayne—they were all beautiful.

Back in the 1920s, now a century ago, it was simple. Developers could just dredge up some good old bay bottomland, seawall it, and make a fortune. The sand basically turned into "gold"! It seemed like a good idea.

The practice slowed in the 1990s, but by 2010, with population soaring, the demand for land became so intense that the rules were eased just a bit, and folks began dredging the bays. Here in 2027, we already have 30 million Crackers, and they're predicting 50 million by 2050. Back in the 1990s, about thirty years ago, rules were so strict that some landowners were unable to develop land they'd been holding for a generation or more.

As the population grew, we suddenly realized the bays themselves were becoming an endangered species. Folks kept moving to Florida. They wanted to live near water—any water—and they flocked into vast complexes of pleasant, uniform shelter-units.

As the real-estate fella was saying to his prospect while describing a piece of old Florida land, "All this needs is some cool water, green trees, and good people to be Heaven." The prospect replied, "Friend, that's all hell needs to be Heaven." Now there's a fella who gets out a lot.

The problem was simply where to put all the people. It was predicted back in the 1970s. It's hard to realize that's fifty years ago. People began to hear about the old Florida doubling game, where population doubled every couple of decades. Everyone knew it would eventually stop. It just never did.

Some old-timers remember when the only way to get across old Lower Tampa Bay was on that old car ferry. It took about an hour and cost about a buck for your car and all the people you could squeeze in.

Folks in every area knew that their bay was the most beautiful of them all. Tampa Bay was always one of the prettier ones. Along about 2005, some developers got the first permits and started dredging . . . at first, just along the Skyway approaches. First thing folks realized, the approaches were almost a mile wide, with about fifty thousand people living there. That's when folks knew it was exactly what had happened across the peninsula of St. Petersburg in Boca Ciega and Boca Grande bays over sixty years before. They just kept gradually dredging more land and shrinking Florida's beautiful bays.

About 2000 is when folks from the Midwest "discovered" North Florida—Apalachicola, Panama City, Pensacola, and all those little bays along the coast—and this area began to fill up with people, just as had happened to South Florida a century before. New roads and cars made the area an easy, pleasant one-day's drive from about half the Midwestern U.S.

But, back to Tampa Bay. At the northern end of that "Grand Old Bay" were the ancient towns of Oldsmar and Safety Harbor. By 2015, dredged bay bottomland stretched over three miles south into the bay. New cities on this land included South Oldsmar and New Safety Harbor, which looked northward into the original towns platted almost two hundred years back.

An outstanding use of bayfront "fill" at St. Petersburg created vast land space. Here can be seen the Maritime Institute, the University of South Florida Bayboro Campus, Albert Whitted Airport, Bayfront Convention Center, downtown yacht docks, and Vinoy Park Hotel in the distance. (Courtesy Florida Department of Commerce/ Tourism Division, photo by Robert Overton)

Miami, the world's leading cruise-ship port, can process thousands of passengers and many ships all at the same time, and does, almost every weekend. (Courtesy Port of Miami)

The original towns had long since disappeared under vast tracts of shelter-units, housing some of the 10 million people living in the megacity of Tampa Bay. (These included, of course, the needy who lived in the highway-buildings under the elevated roads, which by the 2050s would encircle much of the Eastern U.S.; Florida was simply showing the way.) Tampa Bay was not alone. It was just one of the first of the great bays to go on the auction block as part of Florida's seascape for 1,000,000 years simply got filled in, shrunken by about a third, and covered over with buildings and people.

It was nothing new. The Skyway fill was just like Miami's old Biscayne Bay Islands and Tampa's Davis Islands in the land boom. By the 2010s, the only way you could get to those waterfront homes was by small boat; the dredging had left only narrow, little canals where the open bays had been.

Here in the 2020s, Crackers have gotten used to the new E-roads, those sixteen-lane beauties with the electronic beams down the inner lanes. Scientists predicted all this for 100 years ahead, but with 30 million folks and 24 million cars, they became a necessity.

Some folks remember the bays. . . .

Here in the 2020s, Crackers have all grown accustomed to the megamalls, 5,000-car parking lots, our smaze and smog, computerized toll booths, even Maglev trains.

By the 2000s, Florida grew accustomed to investor-owned roads. Critics began questioning the "deals" cut by the state, giving big chunks of land to road builders, just as they'd done with the rail barons nearly two hundred years before. But this time, with 30 million Crackers, roads were an imperative.

Florida—like the rest of America—had to stop and recall. The grand old interstate system was now almost a hundred years old.

Master planning was the key. One plan said that by 2030, Miami's airport would be just ten minutes from the business district—by telephone. Now, that's planning.

Florida had long since become an international community. World corporate offices bloomed all over the state. Her immigrants, back in 2010, included Japanese, German, English, and Swiss, but these were dwarfed by the Latin American influx; Hispanics from the entire hemisphere seeking a new life. All recreated the ancient Florida doubling game.

By 2010, Florida could look back on a fifty-year track of growth, up almost 10 percent in some years . . . but even at an annual rate of 2 percent, it still came out to about a thousand new Crackers every day! Folks don't retire to Chicago or Duluth, and they don't usually have a second home in Green Bay, but they do in Florida. By the 1990s, people were coming from all directions. In southeast Florida, 18 percent—the largest single group of new Crackers—came from one area, Greater New York City. A distant second were natives of the state. Only 12 percent of folks in this corner were from this corner. And 11 percent were folks from New Jersey, so about a third of all southeast Florida people were from New York and New Jersey. Another segment was a mix of Cuban, Jamaican, Canadian, and English; it was an international place.

By the 2010s, Crackers were used to the solid urban sprawl from Miami to Jacksonville; a 360-mile-long town, filled with people.

They said we'd have 20 million people by 2020—we hit that in 2004. They said 30 million by 2040—we hit that last year in 2026. They said women would outlive men; by age eighty-five, there'd be seven women for every man. (Of course it's a little late, guys. Just thought you'd like to know.)

People just kept coming, filling the coastal corridors first and then the cross-state "belts." The Theme Park Capital of the World alone, some thirty miles wide, housed over two million people by 2015. With crowds came trash. Crackers were told of a $50 billion environmental cleanup plan that might take a half-century to complete.

Back in the 1990s, Florida's most densely populated area was in Pinellas County, with various estimates reporting thousands of persons per square mile. To check it out, just spend a month someday on "Old 19," meandering from Maximo Pont to WeekiWatchee Springs.

For real futurists, imagine even 1,000 PPSM, spread over the entire state, and you have 57 million people, spread over the 57,000 square miles of Florida. Now, if you project a growth rate of 2 percent per year, this is about what population would be by 2090. The good news is that while

Cairo, Egypt has 250,000 PPSM, they've been at it for about 6,000 years, so we still have a margin for error, and still have a "ways to go."

Remember that thousand new folks per day? Well, of that group, about one hundred of them were coming to Palm Beach County, making it the #1 growth county in the nation through the 1990s. Another fifty were coming into Dade and Broward counties, another fifty or so were coming into Lee/Ft. Myers and Duval/Jacksonville, and Patrick Carr reported over three hundred were migrating into the Tampa Bay area.

It is now painfully obvious how town founders in Florida before the 1920s often failed to plan ahead. Waterfront lands along the coasts, waterways, lakes, bays, and bayous were forever lost to the people. In town after town we detect lost treasures: a mile-long waterway drive that should have been six miles long; or no avenue where there should have been a beautiful boulevard for a whole town to enjoy and show off to visitors; or a bay-view drive that will never be; or a beautiful, open lake vista magically becoming residential lots and canals. The malady infected virtually every waterfront community that existed in Florida by the 1920s.

By the mid-1990s, Florida's "new generation" of planners began to have their say. New concepts and creations began to reshape old Florida. One has only to view the classic Judy Jacobsen picture of Jacksonville's Landing to grasp Florida's future in the palm of one's hand. Miami's Bayside; Pensacola's Seville Square; Bayfront in Panama City; Orlando's downtown Plazas; Ft. Myers' Riverfront; restored Town Square in St. Augustine, going back 400 years; Old School Square in Delray Beach, restoring the town's 1913 schools; and Tallahassee's Adams Common are just the tip of the iceberg. There are a thousand communities showing the way to tomorrow. Hundreds more will change the face of Florida.

Back around 1999, our two biggest problems were water and our own waste, and we're talkin' garbage . . . big time! A report said we were spending $300 million a year just to dispose of plastic diapers. And somebody said that with the water problems, maybe we could invent a new thing:

The Orlando area's exploding growth, beltways, and commercial development along the International Highway create virtually another new city. (Courtesy Florida Department of Commerce/Tourism Division)

dehydrated water. If you need some, just add some. But it didn't work.

Speaking of trash, Florida's beaches "got trashed" from time to time as unthinking crowds grew blind to these unique treasures. Back in the 1980s, some fifteen thousand volunteer workers got together and picked up 200 tons of garbage from their beaches—just along the lower Atlantic and Gulf coasts alone. Much of the debris turned out to have been thrown overboard from cruise ships along the coasts. With Florida already the cruise-ship capital of the world, this, too, became a major concern.

The good news is that, by the 1990s, the newer ships had developed an "onboard cooker," an incinerator that literally cooked garbage without generating smoke or external heat. Just a fine, white ash remained. And, while doing all this, it actually helped generate power to run the ship's desalination plant, making fresh water out of salt water during the cruise. Ship people tell us the whole "cooker" represents about $70,000 in cost.

Maybe someday we could have one of these gadgets on every street corner in our towns. Just throw in your trash and it helps distill water for us at the same time that it's solving our garbage problem. It's probably better than spending $50 billion over fifty years on cleanup!

At the turn of the millennium, there were plenty of problems to go around; among the leaders were water, waste, and our population.

Back in the 1990s, major companies were developing systems to drive our waste deep into the earth, far below our water aquifers, down 3,500 feet. With this system of "injection wells," said the planners, each county would be able to contract for its own waste system according to its own needs, digesting its own refuse, far below the earth's surface. Apparently the storage was good for the next thousand years or so.

And the really good news was that with that little "cooker" and our giant injection wells combined, there was hope that we might be able to save some of what generations of Cracker kids knew only as—the beach (along with pickin' up the garbage, of course). It's still better than that dehydrated water plan, and it beats that $50 billion idea, too.

WE COULD HAVE A GREAT FUTURE
TO LOOK BACK ON

It's the year 2030, and that bridge we were going to cross when we got to it . . . is here! Our experts have a handle on some of our problems: earth warming, beach nourishment, rising tides, ozone-layer "holes," along with our old standbys, waste, water, and people.

A hundred years ago, engineers warned folks against "grading down the dunes." Folks graded down the dunes, and sure enough, the next generation was spending millions to restore the beaches.

And by the 2020s, plans were underway to begin moving roads and buildings back, to get away from the tides. Folks began to study that whole new phenomenon, earth warming. With earth warming having raised average temperatures about two degrees annually, well below the four to eight degrees scientists predicted, more rain fell and water became less of a problem, but rising seas were an entirely different matter.

However, as scientists pointed out, an annual increase in sea level of only two inches would result, by 2040, in a horizontal movement of 50 to 100 feet in sea tides along Florida's coasts. Her beaches and tides could move inland by 50 to 100 feet.

And finally, a fifty-foot tidal movement would mean: A) Land connections to and through Florida's Keys would be cut off. B) Mangrove plants could likely drown, ending a 1,000-year tour of duty to Florida by the incredible, land-producing plants. C) A wide tongue of salt water would likely move northward through the Everglades, creating a vast, shallow bay. D) With shorelines moving, cities would have to move. If Miami were to expand twenty miles westward, and Naples twenty miles eastward, the "middle" would become a long bridge over what used to be the entire watershed area of the wetlands, about thirty miles wide. E) We would eventually see a solid urban area all the way across South Florida.

You know, with melting polar ice caps and rising seas, it's a good thing those E-roads were about thirty miles inland.

While many landmasses on Earth in similar latitudes as Florida are marked by desert, scientists compared Florida to the Netherlands, with one exception—her most famous home-grown export, hurricanes. The 1928 storm, blowing over Lake Okeechobee, leaving nearly three thousand dead, is one to remember. Should such a blow strike Florida, say, in 2030-40, damage and deaths would be multiplied a hundred-fold. No purpose is served by imagining in these pages such a storm.

In the 1990s, planners were studying tomorrow's list of concerns: air pollution, drainage, flooding, landfills (see Patrick Carr's book, *Sunshine States,* the definitive work on landfills), wetlands, and of course, water, waste, and population. But a new problem was about to enter the "Most Wanted" solution list—traffic.

As we moved into the 2000s, all our problems were inter-connected. Statisticians kept talking of growth-slowdown. For years, Florida had sometimes seen up to a 10 percent population growth within a single year . . . businesses counted on it. In the 1990s, it flattened out to about 2 percent per year, but with all those new Crackers every day, it still meant about six hundred additional cars per day. And that, coupled with over a thousand new cars coming out of showrooms every day . . . well, it was certainly never boring.

They say we used a car for about every 1.8 persons. It just seems you get behind one of those ".8s" every time you hit the road. This also means that if you want to cross the street, you better do it right away. As a matter of fact, with a vehicle crossing the state line every six seconds, it might be better for you just to be born over here.

THE AGE OF SEMINARS

In the 1970s and 1980s, we had many seminars and meetings to talk about our future Florida. People would say, "We're gonna face serious problems," and "We'll see a decline in greenbelt," and "We'll have demands on our water," and one of the most popular comments, "What we need to do, and what I'm in favor of, is not to stop growth, but to control growth." That was always a big seller.

And some folks just said things like, "What time do we tee off?" and "Did you get us a court?"

Of course, there were thousands of dedicated folks who got right down to solving their problems in their own hometown.

In a Delray Beach zoning meeting, many citizens talked about keeping Florida "like she used to be," each saying, in so many words, "I've been here 5-8-13-17-23-27-32 years (take your pick, they were all covered) and I wish it were like it was when I came." The meeting was stopped cold when local native-son-lawyer-dramatist Ernest Simon spoke, saying, "I'm Ernie Simon. I've been here 62 1/2 years, and I wish it were like it was before you came."

But, back to the seminars. Many of the best talkers would zero in on water, which is always a strong opener. They would move quickly to the Everglades, then do a lateral arabesque to the endangered-species medley. In this, they would often list a dozen or so of Florida's creatures, both good and bad, that have been with us for twenty to thirty million years, but that now, suddenly, are going to disappear.

The fact is, these creatures probably wish it were like it was before we came, too.

And finally, some of the folks would even touch on issues! Maybe garbage would come up, or sewage, and eventually, they would get around to people—people who were going to continue coming to Florida as soon as they heard about it, and who would want their piece of paradise, too.

Nothing will change all that, not meetings, seminars, or even handsomely bound programs (gold lettering on leather comes extra).

To give credit where credit is due, many groups of dedicated Crackers devote countless hours to study and concern on how to make Florida a better place in which to live and raise families . . . both in the present and future. These people are the heart and backbone of our future, as they continue to study what may be termed the basics of Florida.

Along about 2001, Florida began realizing all of the above to be true, and began her famous old doubling game all over again anyway, proving once again that whatever goes around comes around, and another fine old Cracker axiom that says, "No matter what happens, there'll always be someone around who always knew it would."

THE BASICS OF FLORIDA

The basics of Florida have occupied concerned citizens for generations, and baffled other groups who've never really caught on. They include (but are not limited to) certain facts: A) Florida will continue to grow. B) There is little to be done about this—so years of talk at beautiful spas and retreats make no difference in this regard. C) The meetings do, however, provide fine business for Florida's spas and retreats. D) Meetings, however, are sometimes at taxpayers' expense. This comes under the heading of Serious Business. E) . . . and sometimes at the individual's expense (sometimes listed in the minutes as "motion shouted down").

Those meetings really haven't made a dent in our problems, such as waste and overpopulation. In 1990, in just Palm Beach County alone, on just one road, I-95, in just one year, county officials reported that folks threw twenty tons of trash out of their car windows. Reports said it cost the county a half-million dollars just to pick up after these folks . . . on just one road.

And when it comes to crowds, back in the 1870s, some folks actually built a big barbed-wire fence along the Florida-Georgia border. They said it was mainly for cows, but the idea was there, just the same.

In the 1970s, parts of the town of Boca Raton thought about voting a population cap on itself of 100,000 people. It was practically on its way to the courts before wiser heads got it stopped.

In one little town, a consultant sold 'em a study, saying they needed a big car wash in the town. It worked fine 'til the guy who owned the car moved away.

The million-dollar studies always said Florida's growth was ending . . . the old doubling game was history. The folks who moved to town just never read the studies. In 1940, we had about one million folks; by 1950, two million; by 1960, about four million; by 1970 eight million; over nine million in 1980; and thirteen million by 1990. Go figure.

At the same time, Florida had become the number-one retirement state in the nation, with Arizona a distant second. Florida's retirement industry was growing by about a billion dollars each year, from back in 1985 to 1990.

Most of the "people figures" skewed towards the "mature" folks. One estimate said that four to six workers are required to serve the needs of every newly retired person who moves to Florida.

For years, countless studies documented activities of Florida's "seniors": their days on the golf course or tennis courts, evenings dining out, spending habits, resources. They come to Florida with about twenty thousand dollars spending money in ready cash, but together they transfer billions in savings and investments from their home state.

All this meant that agriculture was to take on massive importance. How could we feed Florida's growing population? Back in the 1990s, the legislature set up that ten-year, $3 billion plan to buy up lands and hold on to them. The problem was how to keep funding the plan every year to keep it going.

But we're going to keep on seeing those thousand new Crackers coming along every day for about as far ahead as we can see, and it's not even taking the Binder Boys to do it. It's going to be an interesting experience. Like the old Cracker says, "Experience is what you got left after everything else is gone."

One consultant in a seminar actually told folks the majority of new Crackers were not retirees. He probably doesn't get out a lot.

HOW YOU GONNA KEEP 'EM DOWN ON THE FARM AFTER THEY'VE SEEN THE FARM?

In the 1950s, Florida saw suburbs inventing the shopping center. The drive-in concept was based on America's great romance with the automobile. By 1955, something like every fifth or sixth car made in America was a station wagon.

By 2010, we had grown accustomed to instant voice/visual global contact, robot help at home in the multicultural state of Florida, commerce centers with residential sections within easy walking distance, interurban minitransport between minicities where none had existed previously . . . and people and cities stretching to the horizon.

By 2000, we were sharing experiences from California's previous fifty years of exploding growth: lack of planning, lack of support from government and citizens alike, lack of a lot of things . . . including water. California was reaching her final exams in that great school of experience, while Florida still had options and could learn from California's experiences.

Florida's good news is places—Riverwalk, Seville Square, Old School Square, Wakulla and Silver springs, Adams Common, Natural Caverns, Ocala Horse Country, Ravine Gardens—the list goes on and on. The bad news is us inheriting California's post-World War II problems—traffic gridlock, smog, smaze, urban sprawl, urban blight, and the grand champion of them all, dwindling water resources.

Florida may have adopted its own word for its new way of life, Nimby, along with Yuppie, Yummie, Dink, and the rest. We have our own double-breasted, ruby-throated Nimby, who protests the site of the new landfill, the rehab center, the child-care center, the drug halfway house. . . . You name it, everyone needs it, but not in my backyard. As one commentator said, "You want to see community spirit develop real fast? Just try to put any of these items in any specific neighborhood and watch the folks come together."

Back in the 1990s, folks began to realize it was entirely possible for all Crackers to prosper and progress; for her traditional and ancient "two armed camps" to coexist. All her Crackers could enjoy her natural beauty and economic growth and development all at the same time. The scholars and observers realized that, given time, Florida's folks will get along, and will work out compromise plans to accomplish all of the above.

Simply put, they will have to. Whether it be Paine's Prairie or Paine's Lake, a South Florida scenic canal running the length of the peninsula or of the entire state, or St. Petersburg's fabled streetcars, tomorrow's Waterway Boardwalk in Boynton Beach, or the restoration of Ybor City in Tampa, or Lake City's new Sports Hall of Fame, or even a scenic canal across North Florida—even if it takes another hundred years, it's a big land, and there really is enough to go around.

So if you've noticed that it costs more to park your car than it used to cost to run it; if you agree that the only thing

All important future principles of public space and community planning are reflected in Miami's Bayside. (Photo by Judy Jacobsen Photographic Service, Jacksonville)

With a remarkable similarity to Miami's Bayside, the outstanding "Jacksonville Landing" community gathering place on the mighty St. Johns River also uses Florida's water in a smart way. (Photo by Judy Jacobsen Photographic Service, Jacksonville)

America ever did for the Indian was to name a summer after him; if you feel you at least have some of the answers but nobody ever asks you any of the questions; and if you always have too much month left over at the end of the money, and your take-home pay can't stand the trip; then you're just about ready to handle Florida's tomorrow. We need only look back to Florida's yesterday, and we'll find it's up to us in our Florida today.

Bibliography

Five years of research for *Vic Knight's Florida* included personal interviews, public documents, newspapers, as well as notes and recollections of private citizens. Sources included the Florida State Photographic Archives and Florida Department of Commerce, Tallahassee; the Florida State Historical Society; historical societies in Tallahassee, Pensacola, St. Petersburg, Tampa, Delray Beach, and Boca Raton; Washington, D.C.; NASA; Orlando; Florida Chambers of Commerce in these and other cities; *Florida Trend* magazine; and books listed in the following bibliography, available in many Florida public libraries.

Allen, Rodney F. *Fifty-Five Famous Floridians*. Marceline, Mo.: Walsworth Publishing Co., 1985.

Arsenault, Raymond. *St. Petersburg and the Florida Dream*. Virginia Beach: The Donning Co., 1988.

Beater, Jack. *Pirates and Buried Treasure on Florida Islands*. St. Petersburg: Great Outdoors Publishing Co., 1959.

Bloodworth, Bertha, and Alton Morris. *Places in the Sun*. Gainesville: University Presses of Florida, 1978.

Burnett, Gene M. *Florida's Past*. Sarasota: Pineapple Press, 1986, 1988, 1991.

Carr, Patrick. *Sunshine States*. New York: Doubleday, 1990.

Couch, Ernie and Jill. *Florida Trivia*. Nashville: Rutledge Hill Press, 1990.

Curl, Donald W. *Boca Raton, a Pictorial History*. Virginia Beach: The Donning Co., 1989.

Douglas, Marjory Stoneman. *The Everglades: River of Grass*. St. Simons Island, Ga.: Mockingbird Books, 1974.

Dunn, Hampton: *Wish You Were Here*. St. Petersburg: Byron Kennedy & Co., 1981.

——. *Yesterday's St. Petersburg*. Miami: Seeman Publishing Co., 1973.

Hudson, L. Frank, and Gordon R. Prescott. *Lost Treasures of Florida's Gulf Coast*. St. Petersburg: Great Outdoors Publishing Co., 1973.

Keuchel, Edward F.: *A History of Columbia County*. Tallahassee: Sentry Press, 1981.

Knott, James R.: *Palm Beach Revisited*. Boynton Beach: Star Publishing, 1988, 1989.

Lamme, Vernon. *Florida Lore*. Boynton Beach: Star Publishing, 1973.

McIver, Stuart. *Fort Lauderdale and Broward County*. Woodland Hills, Ca.: Windsor Publications Inc., 1983.

——. *Glimpses of South Florida History*. Miami: Florida Flair Books, 1988.

Metzger, Betty, ed. *History of Kissimmee*. St. Petersburg: Byron Kennedy & Co.

Montpelier, Kathleen. *Florida's Heritage*. Salt Lake City: Gibbs M. Smith, Inc., 1982.

Morris, Allen. *Florida Place Names*. Miami: University of Miami Press, 1974.

Parks, Virginia. *Pensacola: Spaniards to Space Age*. Pensacola: Pensacola Historical Society, 1986.

Smiley, Nixon. *Yesterday's Miami*. Miami: Seeman Publishing Co., 1972.

Tebeau, Charlton W. *A History of Florida*. Coral Gables: University of Miami Press, 1981.

Warnke, James. *Ghost Towns of Florida*. Boynton Beach: Star Publishing, 1971.

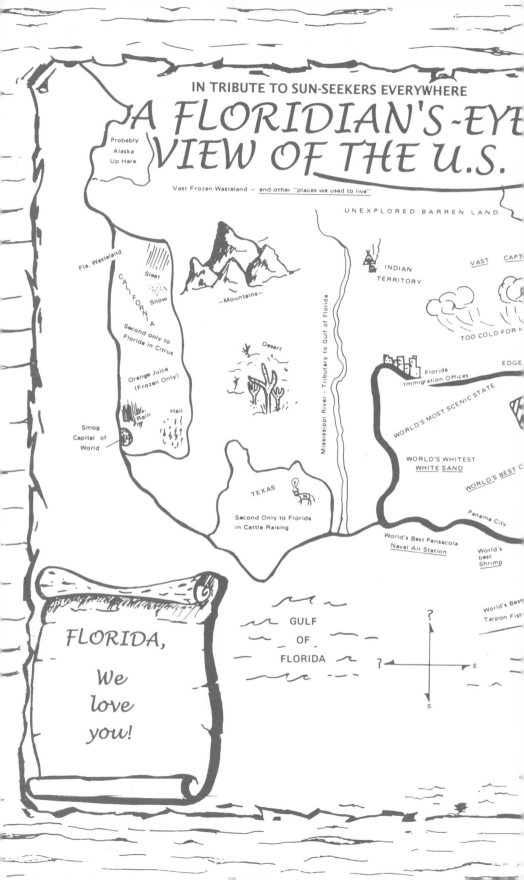